Guaranteed Success

Rewire Your Brain to Rewrite Your Future

Greg Wingard

PINNACLE
BUSINESS
PRESS

Dedication

To Larry Earlywine,
life mentor and dear friend,
whose counsel has proven life-changing.

First Edition. Printed in China.

Wingard, Greg

ISBN 0-9777967-1-X
    1.Success 2. Sales 3. Management
    I. Title

Edited by Dan Johnson and Rosemarie Kowalski

Cover design by Son Duong (sonduong@comcast.net)

Text layout and production by Roberta Great (rgreat@charter.net)

10 9 8 7 6 5 4 3 2 1

CONTENTS

Contents

Your Breakthrough Moment:

*When what you **want** to do becomes **easy** to do*

What do you ache for?

If you could change one thing in your life in the next five years, what would it be?

Take a few moments to think.

To picture. To imagine.

To dream.

Uncork your heart for a moment. What do you *ache* for? If anything—within reason—were possible for you, what would you do in the next five years? Who would you become? What would you accomplish? What would you acquire? What would you contribute?

> *Uncork your heart.*
> *What do you ache for?*

Let me start our conversation with this bold assertion:

> *Unless a man undertakes more than he possibly can do, he will never do all he can do.*
> **Henry Drummond**

You can win almost any prize in life, if you're willing to devote yourself exclusively to it for an extended (but not eternal) period of time.

Guaranteed Success is for those of us who are:

1. *High performers,* who are at the top of our game. We are moving forward, making things happen, reaching higher, and looking for additional strategies to accelerate our performance.

2. *Frustrated* that some of the same goals keep showing up on our

1

list year after year. We want to tackle this challenge by getting in, getting it done, and checking it off the list.

3. *Successful,* but realize the difficulty translating success in some areas into others. Money may come easily to us, but weight loss doesn't. We are tired of this. We want success in the areas where it has eluded us.

Some people are comfortably numb. Life is good for them—but not great. As Jim Collins said in the book, *From Good to Great,* "Good is the enemy of great. And that is one of the key reasons why we have so little that becomes great. We don't have great schools, principally because we have good schools... Few people attain great lives, in large part because it is just so easy to settle for a good life."

Some people are missing their *best* life because they are settling for their *good* life.

But not you.

You're reading a book called *Guaranteed Success* for goodness' sake! You certainly wouldn't be investing your precious time if you didn't aspire to more.

Striving is potent! Henry Drummond said, "Unless a man undertakes more than he possibly can do, he will never do all he can do." Round these words out with the wisdom of Lawrence J. Peter who commented, "Only a mediocre person is always at his best." Clearly, the happiest people on earth are those who savor where they are while *at the same time* hotly pursuing more—more growth, more achievement, more attainment, more contribution.

> *Nearly half of those responding to a Yale University online survey said they would give up a year of their life to be thin.*
> **The Seattle Post-Intelligencer**

In May of 2006, I came across a bizarre—and telling—study. The *Seattle Post-Intelligencer* ran the article at the top of page A10. The title caught my eye and captured my attention:

"They'd trade year of life for a thinner waist."

I had to read the article.

"Nearly half of those responding to a Yale University online survey said they would be willing to give up a year of their life rather than be fat."

There's more: 15% said they would trim a *decade* off their lives for a thinner waist.

Let that sink in.

Is that bizarre, or what?

"Who would do that?" I wondered.

I saved the article. While I was doing research for this book, I came across it again and reread it with bewilderment. This time I put myself in their shoes.

I thought about my goals for the next five years and concluded that I might exchange some of my life to realize a couple of them.

Imagine there was a cosmic "Rewards Program" where someone could exchange *time* for *quality of life*. Choose a goal, and you can have it. All you need to do is cash in a few points. Let's say you are going to die on April 15, 2052. If you could have your most important goal realized *right now*, would you be willing to bump up that final day to April *14*, 2052? Life would end the same way, with the same people around you. It would just end one day earlier. Hey, you could even skip paying taxes that year!

Quite a few people might join the program.

Many would exchange a day of *time* for four decades of a *much higher quality of life*.

Well, what if that exchange required not a day, but a *week*? Would most people make the swap? I think so.

How about a month?
    A year?

Suddenly it doesn't seem so bizarre.

Quality of life matters. It matters a lot.

> *Quality of life matters. It matters a lot.*

3

Whether or not we would make this bizarre, hypothetical switch, an interesting question arises...

Why is it so hard to change?

If we want some things so badly, why is it so darn hard to change?

When I first read about the Yale study in the *Seattle Post-Intelligencer*, I thought, "Why don't those people just go on a diet?"

It quickly dawned on me: they have! They've gone on many of them. They are discouraged because despite their desire, their results have been dismal.

Here's the good news: you don't have to give up a year to reach your most important goal!

Crystal clarity, focus, tenacity, and a handful of vital strategies will give you everything you need to do whatever matters most to you. Right now.

You can lose the weight and keep it off.

You can go from middle of the pack to the next tier in your sales career.

You can take your leadership skills to the next level.

You can turn a good marriage into a great one.

You can quit smoking.

You can break out of the debt cycle and begin creating the wealth you want.

If it really matters to you, you can change—and in changing yourself, you can *guarantee* the success you crave.

Where next?

Take a few minutes to dream a little. Five years from now...

- How do you want to be perceived?
- How do you want to be different than you are today?
- Where do you want to be financially?

4

- What differences would you like to see in your close relationships?
- How do you want to feel physically? What do you want to look like? What kind of energy level do you want to have?
- Where do you want to be in your career?

Pause.

Was that stressful?

Or did it juice you?

When we're in a season of forward momentum, anything seems possible. We frame our future with *possibility*.

When we're in a season of negative momentum, we feel stifled. We frame our future with *limitation*.

> *When we are in a season of forward momentum, anything seems possible. We frame our future with possibility.*

Where are you right now?
Either way…
… *get ready to move forward!*

Take a few more minutes to get clearer. Identify your "Top Five in Five." Within reason, identify five goals you would like to have achieved five years from now.

Identify your "Top Five in Five."

Write the exact date five years from today: _____ .
Within reason, what are the top five goals you would like to have achieved by that date?

1. _____

2. _____

3. _____

4. _____

5. _____

Now...

    ... let me say this—without an ounce of hype:

    you absolutely can achieve all five of those goals in the next five years, if...

IF.

It's a huge "if."

IF you tackle them *one at a time*. If you give each one total focus until you master the beliefs and behaviors that will create *lasting results.*

Think about how we often go about working toward our goals. We have a handful of goals, and we try moving forward incrementally on all of them at the same time. For years, I called this "balance." Yet with this approach, we have trouble making significant and lasting change on any of them.

We move forward only to give up our gains. A perfect example is dieting. Every year, 15-35% of Americans go on diets. Despite short-term success, 90-95% of them regain the weight—and most are heavier than when they started.[1]

    This strategy rarely works.

The reason most people don't break through to new results is because they are attempting too many things at once.

There is a different way.

> *You can achieve all five of your most important goals over the next five years, if you are willing to take them one at a time.*

You *can* achieve all five of your most important goals over the next five years, if...

    ... you are willing to take them one at a time.

Here's how to do it.

Of the five, identify the most important target to tackle first. Then devote yourself exclusively to it. Allow three to six months to identify new beliefs and behaviors that produce the results you want, then focus on those until you literally rewire your brain to think and act at the new level—*automatically.* This will guarantee ongoing results at the new level. Then—and only then—move on.

After you've mastered it, (mastery will *not* take forever—it will just take concentrated focus for an extended period of time) move to the next area and take the same approach.

Take them one at a time, give them the focus needed, and you absolutely can achieve your Top Five in Five.

It's as easy (or as hard) as riding a bicycle

Think back to your childhood.

Do you remember how many new skills you learned in those early years?
Swimming.
Writing in cursive.
Throwing a baseball.
Catching bugs.
Riding a bicycle.

Ah, yes, riding a bicycle.

Do you remember the sheer terror of taking off the training wheels?

Here's a question for you.
Is riding a bicycle easy—or hard?

Answer it before I give you my opinion.

Here's what I think: "It depends."

It depends on whether or not you know how to ride.

For someone who knows how to ride a bike, it's a piece of cake. But for the person who hasn't learned yet, it is exceedingly difficult.

I know this seems obvious, but please note: riding a bicycle is never "kind

7

of hard" or "kind of easy." It is either exceedingly difficult or extremely easy. It's always one or the other.

It all depends on whether or not you have experienced what I call

"The Breakthrough Moment."

The Breakthrough Moment is that point in time when what you *want* to do becomes *easy* to do. It is the point where the skill you've been working on isn't hard to do anymore. It is when you "get it."

What is amazing about The Breakthrough Moment is that it is just that—*a moment*. It doesn't happen gradually—it happens at a point in time.

Here's why.

> *The Breakthrough Moment is that point in time when what you want to do becomes easy to do.*

The Breakthrough Moment happens because of a specific change taking place in the brain. At the Breakthrough Moment a new skill is hardwired into our long-term memory.

Do you remember the moment you stayed on your bike without falling? Before then, it took all of your focus. It took every ounce of concentration to shift your weight, peddle like crazy, hope, pray, and then finally…

…you got it! Suddenly, all that effort streamed together into one fluid motion. Instantly it became easy. After a few minutes, you could look around and notice where you were and who was there. You could think about other things!

When you learned to ride a bike, tie a shoe, use a fork, type on a keyboard, play a musical instrument, or swing a golf club, mastering each new skill involved exactly the same process. When you "got it"—when it became easy to you—something simple, yet profound, took place in your brain:

> *Mastery is not merely "in your head.' It's actually "in your brain."*

The new skill became hard-wired in your long-term memory.

That feeling of mastery is not merely

8

"in your head." It's actually "in your brain."

Your resistance to change is a good thing

Believe it or not, your resistance to change is a good thing.

Here's why. Your resistance to change is your brain's way of protecting the patterns you have worked so hard to establish.

> Believe it or not, your resistance to change is a good thing. Your brain is simply defending the patterns you have worked so hard to establish.

Imagine life the other way.

Imagine having to relearn everything daily. Picture a life where each morning you have to relearn getting dressed, tying your shoes, and brushing your teeth. In that case, you wouldn't have left the house this morning!

Our brain defends the patterns we have worked hard to establish. When we've invested the time, focus, and hard work to learn to tie our shoes, ride a bicycle, connect with someone we've never met, give a great presentation, and invest with savvy, our brains protect those patterns so we can move on and learn new things.

David Rock and Jeffrey Schwartz wrote:

> "Why do people resist change so stubbornly...? New advances in neuroscience provide insight into why change can be so difficult...
>
> The first has to do with the nature of human memory and its relationship to conscious attention. Working memory—the brain's 'holding area,' where perceptions and ideas can first be compared to other information—is frequently engaged when people encounter something new. When you see a new product on a supermarket shelf and rationally compare its benefits to a product you already use, it's your working memory that takes in the new information and matches it against the old. This kind of memory activates the prefrontal cortex, an energy-intensive part of the brain.
>
> The basal ganglia, on the other hand, are invoked by routine, familiar activity, like putting an often-purchased product into a

supermarket cart without consciously paying attention, and perhaps without later remembering having picked it out. This part of the brain, located near the core, is where neural circuits of long-standing habit are formed and held. It requires much less energy to function than working memory does...

The basal ganglia can function exceedingly well without conscious thought in any routine activity. In contrast, working memory fatigues easily and can hold only a limited amount of information 'on line' at any one time. Therefore, any activity conducted repetitively (to the point of becoming a habit) will tend to get pushed down into the basal ganglia, the habit-center part of the brain. This frees up the processing resources of the prefrontal cortex.

After just a few months of learning to drive a car, people can typically drive without thinking. If they then try to drive on the other side of the road, say in another country, the act of driving suddenly becomes much more difficult. The prefrontal cortex must now be used to keep track of the action...

The same cognitive dynamics come into play when people face other types of stressful experiences, including any strategic or organizational change. Much of what managers do in the workplace—how they sell ideas, run meetings, manage others, and communicate—is so well routinized that the basal ganglia are running the show. Trying to change any hardwired habit requires a lot of effort in the form of attention. This often leads to a feeling that many people find uncomfortable. So they do what they can to avoid change."[2]

We have thousands of skills—large and small—hardwired in our brain.

Knowing this helps us work *with* our brain—rather than *fighting* it.

> *Work with your brain instead of fighting it.*

Remember, resistance to change is simply the brain's way of protecting the patterns we have worked so hard to establish.

Our brains are like a medieval castle.

Imagine an imposing stone castle, equipped with steep walls, large cut stones, and an enormous wood-plank gate. Whenever you attempt to establish new patterns, it is as if you have arrived at the castle seeking entry.

You reach for the iron clapper, and begin pounding on the door with all of your might. "Rap! Rap! Rap!"

No response.

You pound again: "Rap! Rap! Rap! Rap!"

No response.

You continue.

Again, no response.

Your brain, seeking to protect all the patterns safely housed inside, resists your entry. It is telling you, "No! We're not letting you in. We're comfortable and cozy in here. Go away!"

You keep rapping.

Your brain keeps saying, "Go away! We're not letting you in!"

But you persist.

You keep rapping... "Rap! Rap! Rap!"

Finally.............

... after continued persistence on your part...

... your brain finally says...

... *"Okay. I see you really want in...*

... "Go ahead and come in."

And the door swings wide.

You walk in.

Then the brain slams the door shut. It locks in the new pattern and protects it just as vigorously as it protects all the other patterns you've worked so hard to establish.

And here's the beauty:

... you have it for life.

Unless you intentionally focus your energy and attention to reverse this new pattern—pounding repeatedly on your brain's door—you have it. For life.

Again, it's just like riding a bicycle.

How long has it been since you've been on one?
A day? A week? A year? A decade?

It doesn't matter.

> *If you focus your attention long enough to "get it," you've got it for life*

If you focused your attention on learning that skill to the point of "getting it," you have it for life. It doesn't matter how long you've gone without riding. Whenever you get back on the bike you will enjoy riding it without having to agonizingly relearn the skill.

You've got it. It is hardwired in your brain's long-term memory. As long as you hold on to your brain, you'll hold on to the skill.

It doesn't matter how long it has been since you've been on a bike. What matters is that you persisted in mastering the skill of riding until you reached...

The Breakthrough Moment

The Breakthrough Moment is that point in time when you "get it." It is where what you *want* to do becomes *easy* to do.

At that moment, the object of your focus becomes hardwired in your long-term memory.

Neuroscientists at John Hopkins University discovered that within five or six hours of learning a new motor skill, learning shifts from the prefrontal cortex (involved in short-term memory) to other parts of the brain that help control movement. Once it is hardwired, subjects can perform the new skill without practice. As Dr. John Ratey says in *A User's Guide to the Brain,* "This suggests that a newly learned skill could be impaired, confused, or even lost if a person tried to learn a different motor task during the critical 5-to-6 hour period, when the brain is trying to stabilize the neural representation and retention of the original task."[3]

It doesn't matter how long it has been since you learned a new skill. What matters is that you persist in your mastery of the new skill until it becomes hardwired into your long-term memory.

The key is persisting until you reach that Breakthrough Moment.

How long did you need to focus on learning to ride a bike?
As long as it took to "get it."

Imagine quitting before you "got it."

It took me a long time to learn to ride, but I was motivated! I wanted to ride to 7-11 on my own bike and buy Jolly Ranchers with my allowance money. At the time, Evil Knievel was jumping cars on his motorcycle. I wanted to learn so we could set up ramps and jump over things on our bike. The most fun was laying our friends in between the ramps, jumping four or five at a time!

Like you, I endured many frustrating days—and lots of scrapes and bruises. It took hours of practice.
But I got it.

Imagine quitting right before that Breakthrough Moment.

What if I threw my hands up and said, "Dad, I'm done. That's the last time I am leaving my skin on the pavement. Maybe I'll take this up when I'm in my twenties."

How sad it would have been and how much fun I would have missed.

If I came back to it as a 24-year-old, I'd have to start from scratch.

My brain's working memory would have moved on. The work would have been lost. If I wanted to "get it" and make riding a bike easy, I'd have to relearn the skill and stick with it until the Breakthrough Moment.

Here's a question:
In learning how to ride a bicycle, when is a person most discouraged?

Guaranteed Success

Think about it.

Here's when:

Right before the Breakthrough Moment.

After trying for days and failing over and over again, after multiple scrapes and bandages, that's when they are most tempted to throw in the towel.

And yet...
... that is when they are closest to the Breakthrough Moment.

They may be just a few hours—or just 60 seconds—away.
One thing's certain: they are *much closer* than when they began. Although *it feels* like they are further away.

This can change your life!

It has changed mine.

This insight into how we can work with our brain to produce lasting change is, by far, the most powerful tool I have encountered to create breakthrough change and rapidly accelerate performance.

I don't say this lightly. I read scores of books a year and continually scour the landscape for insights that will produce peak performance.

This insight—and mastering a handful of strategies to leverage this insight for accelerated change—can change your life!

Guaranteed Success is full of hope.

But it is much more.

Guaranteed Success is a strategy to create lasting, breakthrough results through creating lasting, breakthrough change in *you*. The principles of *Guaranteed Success* are grounded firmly on the time-tested fundamentals of peak performance and enriched by the latest findings of modern neuroscience.

14

Guaranteed Success will demystify why some things comes easily to you while others don't. *Guaranteed Success* will also demystify why some of your change efforts have

> *Guaranteed Success provides the missing link between your desire for new results and your achievement of new results.*

succeeded and others haven't. It will provide the missing link between your *desire* for new results and your *achievement* of those new results.

Most importantly, *Guaranteed Success* will provide a clear and simple road-map to the results you want long-term. It will inspire and it will instruct. It will fire up your heart and provide light for your path. It will reawaken you to the possibilities of your life—and will provide you tools to turn those possibilities into reality.

At one level, *Guaranteed Success* will provide you a *new* way to win *old* battles. And at another level, *Guaranteed Success* will supply you with the outlook, the knowledge, and the tools to go from success to success—to seize new opportunities and tackle new challenges that previously seemed out of reach.

As a coach, my goal is to do whatever it takes to get you to the next level. I will not hold back! Your life it too valuable—and your future too full of potential—for me to play it safe with you!

Your life may be good. But it is about to get better.

A mentor of mine used to say, "None of us is getting A's in everything." Carl Jung said, "The normal man is a fiction." I love what Rodney Dangerfield added, "The

> *Your life may be good. But it is about to get better.*

only normal people are the ones you don't know too well."

Again, your life may be good. But it is about to get better.

Imagine a future…

Without diets. Without weight loss goals. Imagine getting beyond the obsession with weight. Imagine being able to take all of that energy and apply it to other things!

Imagine a future…

Without financial stress. Without credit card debt. Without arguments over spending. Imagine enjoying what you have while having a sense of control. Imagine being happy where you are while being confident that you are moving forward on your financial goals. Imagine feeling like your financial house is in order and you are ready for anything that comes.

Imagine a future…

Where you are at the top of your career game. Where you are performing near peak potential, and where you are continuing to grow, develop, and become more skilled. Where you are fully in control of your career path.

Imagine a future…

Where family relationships are not stagnant or deteriorating, but getting better every year. Where time is your friend. Where time means ever-improving communication, growing intimacy, the creation of fantastic memories, and the weaving together of your lives into a tapestry.

All these and much more are fully available to you.

But please remember this:

the key to achieving these exciting prizes is taking them *one at a time*.

I want to tantalize you!

But I also want to steady you.

For us to accelerate our performance, we must focus intensely—and that means setting aside many important things in order to focus on that which is most important now.

I am here to coach you. To challenge you. To encourage you. To provide you the tools.

You absolutely *can* do extraordinary new things in your life. It's up to you. Seize it. Own it. Make it happen.

You can change.

Your good life can be even better.

It is possible.

For you.
Right now.

> *One cannot teach a man anything.*
> *One can only enable him to learn*
> *from within himself.*
> **Galileo (1564-1642)**

If you'll focus, lasting change is easier than you think.

> *People don't need to be managed, they*
> *need to be unleashed.*
> **Richard Florida (2002)**

Your best days are ahead.

Guaranteed Success—in a paragraph

Here is what *Guaranteed Success* is all about:

1. Within reason, you can change—and achieve—almost anything in your life.

   > *Yes, it's that simple.*

2. Results flow from your *habitual* beliefs and behaviors.
3. The key to better results is rewiring your beliefs and behaviors to get better results *automatically.*
4. The key to rewiring your brain is focusing almost exclusively, for an extended (but not eternal) period of time, on new beliefs and behaviors until they get hardwired in your brain.

Yes, it's that simple.

> *How to contact the author:*
> *Greg Wingard*
> *Founder and CEO, Simple Team Solutions*
> *gregw@simpleteamsolutions.com*

Guaranteed Success

The New Science of High Performance:

Stop fighting your brain—rewire it instead

It's not about what you know

Think about your top target.

What will it take to create lasting change and long-term success with that target?

Here's a surprise:

You already have enough information.

In fact, don't you think you could probably know *half* what you know now, and still achieve your goal?

For most, just having more information doesn't break long-standing patterns of low performance. If anything, our abundance of information merely increases guilt.

Take weight loss, for example.

It seems that every week another study emerges. Pick the week and you'll hear an authority wax eloquent on the obesity epidemic. Off the top of my head, I have seen studies, research reports, or articles on all of these topics over the past month:

> *More information doesn't usually help us change. It just makes us feel guilty.*

- There are now more obese people in China than starving people.
- More than 60% of Americans are overweight.
- We have a growing obesity epidemic in children—and diabetes is skyrocketing because of it.
- Most people gain five pounds during the holidays.

- People who are even mildly overweight will die one to four years earlier than if they were fit.
- 90-95% of people who go on diets gain all the weight back—and more.

It's depressing, isn't it? It makes you want to reach for a jelly-filled Krispy Kreme doughnut to ease the pain!

Here's an irony: we are fatter than our parents and our grandparents, but they were able to enjoy things like hamburgers and biscuits and gravy! We have more information, but poorer habits and, as a result, have trouble enjoying our splurges.

> *You probably already know what to do. What you don't know is how to make doing it automatic.*

Please, get this.

You probably already know what to do.

What you don't know is how to make doing it *automatic.*

That's the whole ballgame right there.

And that is what *Guaranteed Success* is all about.

I can help you! This book, this process, and the many *Guaranteed Success* programs and seminars we offer, can absolutely help you utilize what you know. We can help you do what you want to do *automatically.* And in doing so, we can help guarantee long-term success.

Again, *Guaranteed Success* will help you…
1. Use what you already know.
2. Replicate your success.
3. Make doing what you want *automatic.*

Why do smart people underperform?

Why are some achievements relatively easy and others stubbornly difficult?

Why do so many change efforts fail?

I don't want to be depressing!
    I'm just being real.

About a year ago, I was working on my quarterly goals, and I had a sickening realization: I had a few goals that had reappeared on my goals list for more than a decade!

One of those goals was weight loss. Despite success in "all things career," the excess weight was a stubborn tenant. No matter what I did, I just couldn't get it to leave!

I exercised regularly, tried to "be good" with my eating, and (to my wife) appeared obsessed with weight, food, and eating. But I fluctuated between being 25-40 pounds over my recommended weight. As I reviewed my goals at a Starbucks in early 2006, I realized that weight loss had appeared on my list *as early as 1995*! That, my friend, was disheartening!

As I reflected on years of intense effort, it was as if I was fighting my own "Vietnam War"—always engaged in it, never totally committed to it, never winning it, and always frustrated by it. The struggle went on and on and on.

You probably have an area or two like that in your life.

How can we be wildly successful in some areas, while having difficulty translating success to other areas? Why do we rapidly advance in an area, then hit a plateau or face a wall that stubbornly refuses to yield to our desire for continual advancement?

> *It is not necessary to change. Survival is not mandatory.*
> **W. Edwards Deming**

Why do so many people live far below their potential?

Why are so many a lot smarter than their results indicate?

Those questions drove—and ultimately led—me to some of the most exciting and important performance discoveries of my life! As Morpheus said to Neo in *The Matrix*, "It is the question that drives you." It drove

> *Smart people hate feeling dumb. Fast people hate feeling slow. Developing new and better habits requires both.*

me, leading me to some huge discoveries!

Here are several reasons why smart people sometimes underperform:

- They are busy but unfocused.
- They become cynical.
- They belong to a generation of smarts specialists.
- They believe that information alone is power.
- They are fast—and hate being slow.
- They are smart—and hate feeling dumb.
- They think change is more complicated than it really is.

> *In a corporate environment that is changing at warp speed, performing consistently at high levels is more difficult and more necessary than ever.*
> **Jim Loehr and Tony Schwartz**

Here are some smart insights for smart people:

1. *Focus is a must.* For reasons that will become very clear, we absolutely must narrow our focus. Accelerate by slowing down. Attempt less and accomplish more. This is a huge differentiator for accelerated performance in our current hurried environment.

2. *Reject cynicism.* It only pays if you're a comic. Most of us have laughed at Al Franken's goofy character, Stuart Smalley, who is a caricature of a performance specialist. His mantra, "I'm good enough, I'm smart enough, and gosh darn it, people like me!" pokes fun at peak performance tools like goal-setting, affirmations, and the ability to direct our lives. Be careful! Cynicism pays Al Franken well—but it can kill your potential! I enjoyed laughing at Stuart, but too much of that stuff is toxic. Flee cynicism. It corrodes!

3. *Know what you don't know.* Be a learn-it-all, rather than a know-it-all.

4. *Don't just hear information—apply it.* Hearing does not equal knowing. Some people think that because they have heard something before, they know it. A person doesn't know something until they've *lived* it—until they've *experienced* it. Think about your

area of expertise. If someone reads an article about it and spouts some of the terms, do they "know" it like you do? Of course not. Hearing does not equal knowing. Information is not power. Everyone who has heard of a

> *Information is not power. Everyone with access to the Internet has access to the world's information. Information is not power. Applied information is power.*

thing called the Internet has access to all of the world's information. Information is not power. *Applied* information is power.

Ah, applied information.

That is life changing.

5. *Embrace the awkwardness of learning new stuff.* Remember this: if we never feel dumb, we're not learning anything new!

6. *Give up the myth of "the natural."* Many people have been lulled into mediocrity because they stand in awe of those who make excellence look easy. But people who look like "naturals" have worked their butts off to get there. Thomas Edison said "Genius is 99% perspiration and 1% inspiration." When Muhammad Ali defeated Sonny Liston, he upset the experts. *Liston*—not Ali—was "the natural." Michael Jordan's famous "cut" from his high school team is legend. Wilma Rudolph was hailed as the fastest woman on earth after she won three gold medals in the 1960 Rome Olympics. The backstory is that at age four, she nearly died of pneumonia, scarlet fever, and polio, and emerged with a leg that was almost paralyzed. The experts said she'd never use it again. After her unbelievable career, she said, "I just want to be remembered as a hardworking lady." Give up the myth of "the natural." There is no such thing.

7. *Keep it simple.* Guy Kawasaki warned against being "too smart to start." It's really not that complicated. A few key changes, rigorously applied, will get you where you want to go next. Look for the simple things, the life-changing things. Keep it simple.

> *Faced with the choice between changing one's mind and proving that there is no need to do so, almost everyone gets busy on the proof.*
> **John Kenneth Galbraith**

Vincent Van Gogh said, "Do not quench your inspiration and your imagination; do not become the slave of your model."

Dream.

Think bigger.

You can do *far more* than you realize.

Learn like Tiger

Golfer Tiger Woods is one of the great athletes of our time. Recently, I heard a commentator muse on air, "Is Tiger Woods bad for golf?" His reasoning: Tiger was moving so far ahead of the pack that it was taking the fun out of golf for the fans.

What an athlete!
What a commitment to peak performance.
In a league all by himself.

How did he get there?
1. He vigorously seeks coaching.
2. He repeatedly pulls his game apart piece by piece and relentlessly improves it.

> *The best in the world are always the most vigorous learners.*

The best performers in the world are always the most vigorous learners. Find a person who excels and you'll find someone who asks questions, gets coaching, finds ways to get better, and always makes positive changes. She is a "learn-it-all."

> *Great leaders are never satisfied with current levels of performance. They constantly strive for higher and higher levels of achievement.*
> **Donna Harrison**

Find someone who has plateaued and you'll discover a person who thinks he already knows it all, can figure it out himself, resents those who are highly successful, and is stuck in his ways. He is a "know-it-all."

Like Tiger…

24

1. Get coached.
2. Take your "game" apart, and master each part, piece by piece.

Be open. Be humble. Be a learn-it-all. Savor your wins but never be satisfied.

Learn like Tiger.

A user's manual for your brain

How many user's manuals do you have?

If you scrounged around your garage, office, files, and cupboards, I bet you could find a dozen. We've got user's manuals for cars, microwaves, and Blackberries. Every piece of clothing, cord, and string of Christmas lights comes with a little tag of care instructions.

Yet you and I possess the most complex piece of equipment in the galaxy. It is *far* more complex than any piece of equipment produced by an American, Chinese, German, or Japanese company. GE can't touch it and neither can Google. If you combined the accumulated know-how of nanotechnology, biotechnology, and computer programming, it would be a fraction as sophisticated as the equipment to which I'm referring.

Of course, I am talking about the human brain.

You've got one.

But it didn't come with a user's manual.

Here are some "fast facts" about the human brain:[4]
1. It weighs three pounds.
2. It burns 20% of your daily calorie intake.
3. Your brain is, by far, the most complex object in the known universe.
4. It comprises one hundred billion neurons, and ten times as many other cells that have noncomputational roles.
5. Each neuron may have anywhere from one to 10,000 synaptic connections to other neurons.

6. That means the theoretical number of different potential connections in a single brain is roughly 40,000,000,000,000,000— forty quadrillion.

7. The brain has the long-term storage capacity of 6 million years of the *Wall Street Journal*.

8. Your short-term memory is very energy-intensive. This is why after a day of intense learning or stress, you find yourself physically exhausted.

9. The brain's short-term memory can hold just seven (plus or minus two) pieces of information at a time.

Isn't that mind-boggling?

> *Memory is learning that sticks. Before memory, potential new learning lingers briefly in a kind of "scratchpad" about the size of a postage stamp that is located in the right prefrontal cortex, above the right eye and about one inch behind the forehead. This working-memory area can hold the proverbial seven, plus or minus two bits, of information until such time as we decide to make a permanent record of it.*
>
> **Pierce J. Howard, Ph.D.**

And yet we didn't receive a user's manual with our brain. If we did, here are some things it might have contained:

1. Short-term memory is a distinct function of the brain—and is extremely limited.

2. Long-term memory is virtually unlimited. You will run out of life centuries before you run out of long-term memory.

3. When we feel overwhelmed, we are overloading our *short-term* memory, not our long-term memory.

4. When a new skill moves from short-term to long-term memory, it becomes hard-wired.

5. Since short-term memory is the constraining factor in our brain's development, the key to accelerated change is understanding how to properly use our short-term memory.

6. Going half-way doesn't help. If we focus on a new skill for awhile— but not long enough to create a long-term memory—we lose it once we switch focus.

7. New long-term memories are a rewiring of the brain.
8. A rewired brain will think and act at the new level automatically.

Here's a bit of sobering—and empowering—news:

You are not getting what you *want*. You are getting what your brain is *wired* for.

> *You are not getting what you want. You are getting what your brain is wired for.*

Change your wiring—and you *will* change your results.

Script new beliefs.

Sculpt new behaviors.

Rewire your brain to think and act at the next level…

… and you *will* change your results.

Guaranteed.

Pictures of breakthrough change

The more ways we visualize how to change, the easier it is to envision doing it.

It helps us to focus. It helps us persist.

What does breakthrough change look like?

Resetting the thermostat

As I write this, I'm sitting in a room where the thermostat is set at 70 degrees. If the room temperature drops to 68, the heater will kick in and bring it back up to 70. If the temperature pops up to 72, the air conditioning will roar into action pulling it back down to 70. The thermostat is not committed to cold or heat. It is committed to maintaining the programmed temperature. Our brains operate the same way. Our brain doesn't care if our habits help or hinder us. Our brain simply obeys our decisions. It wants

27

to form patterns as quickly as possible so it can move on and help us learn new things.

> *Our brain doesn't care if our habits help or hinder us. Our brain simply obeys our decisions.*

If we want hotter results, we simply must reset the thermostat to a higher temperature. When we do that, our brains maintain the new temperature just as vigorously.

Living on autopilot

Another way to picture breakthrough change is by changing our autopilot. Harv Eker says, "Most of us believe that we live our lives based on choice. Not usually! Even if we're really enlightened, we might make just a few choices during the average day that reflect our awareness of ourselves in the present moment. But for the most part, we're like robots, running on automatic, ruled by our past conditioning and old habits."

Think about all that your brain is doing for you right now—without conscious awareness. Your amazing brain is regulating body temperature and monitoring your blood flow. It is processing the words on this page while you breathe, look, and turn the page. As you navigate your day, most things are done automatically. Answering a cell phone, getting behind the wheel of a car, ordering lunch, or firing off an email will be done quickly and effortlessly. We live largely on autopilot. The secret to better results is improving our autopilot.

From mental RAM to your hard-drive

John Ratey describes short-term memory this way: "Short-term memory acts like a computer's RAM: it holds the data we are working with at the moment, but loses them once the machine is turned off. Long-term memory acts like the computer's hard disk: information is only put there when we hit "Save," but once it's put there it stays there so that we can access it again and again."[5]

Many people overload their RAM—and in doing so hinder its ability to convert learning to long-term memory. Every failed diet is an example of putting something on the brain's RAM, without persisting until the new behaviors became hardwired into long-term memory. The key to breakthrough change is being more selective about what we put on our RAM, and then staying with that focus until our brain converts the learning to long-term memory.

Letting the cement dry

When we make improvements, it is as if we are laying forms and pouring cement. As the project takes shape, it initially excites us. After the cement is poured, it is boring waiting around for the cement to dry. Yet dry it must. When people quit on a change before they've ingrained it into new habits, they are leaving the project site before the cement has dried. Persistence is simply the act of allowing the cement to dry so we can enjoy the results of our work, long-term.

Writing your story

You are living a story. Whose story is it? You think about your story, talk about your story, and interpret everything through the filter of your story. You have a story line about where you came from, where you're going, and what you can accomplish.

> *You are living a story. Whose story is it?*

When you choose to focus and change something in your life, you are choosing to rewrite part of the story. When you rewrite your story, you own the rights. It is *your* story, and the narrative is under construction.

Rewiring your brain

When we create breakthrough change, we are literally rewiring our brain. We are strengthening synaptic connections, creating new ones and even growing new neurons. We are laying new cables in our brain.

> *We can't fight against our brain. But we can rewire it. Rewiring our brain is the quickest way to lasting change.*

We can't *fight* against our brain. But we can *rewire* it. And therein lies virtually unlimited potential for growth, change, and accelerated results.

Your adult brain can change!

One of the most important—and exciting—scientific breakthroughs of our time is that the adult brain can change.

For decades, neuroscientists believed the human brain was hardwired during childhood and that substantive change was impossible. As Jeffrey Schwartz writes, "This doctrine of the adult hard-wired brain, of the loss of neuroplasticity with the end of the childhood, had profound ramifications. It implied that rehabilitation for adults who had suffered brain damage was useless. It suggested that cognitive rehab in psychiatry was a misbegotten dream. But the doctrine… was wrong…."[6]

> *Genes do not make a man… violent, or fat, or a leader. Genes merely make proteins… Genes are overruled every time an angry man restrains his temper, a fat man diets, and an alcoholic refuses to take a drink.*
> **John J. Ratey, M.D.**

Two significant breakthroughs helped overturn the old dogma of the hardwired adult brain.

One of the breakthroughs is widely known: stroke patients have been able to overcome learned nonuse of a limb. The other breakthrough is less known: sufferers of obsessive-compulsive disorder have been able to overcome their obtrusive thoughts through mindfulness practice. In both, literal brain remapping takes place.

The bottom line?

You and I are not stuck.

Our brains can change!

Since adult brains can adapt, change, and grow throughout life, there are a few notions we need to dispel. None of these is true—although each has probably rolled off our tongue a time or two:

1. "I'm not good at that."
2. "That's not me."
3. "It's too late."

Replace those outdated ideas with these facts grounded in neuroscience:

1. "I'm good at whatever I wire myself to be good at."
2. "I am whatever I choose to become."
3. "I can grow and change throughout my entire lifetime."

It almost seems too good to be true.

But it's not.

It's true.

Accept your limitations *and* embrace your potential

The brain is an instrument of possibilities, not certainties.

When it comes to investing in neural real estate, the rich really do get richer, and the poor get poorer.

> *The brain is an instrument of possibilities, not certainties.*

Embrace your potential:

You have almost limitless possibilities for attainment, change, and growth. You will run out of life centuries before you will run out of capacity for growth.

At the same time, accept your limitation:

There is a real limit to your short-term memory. You can only focus on a few things, if you hope to create lasting, long-term brain change. *While you have almost unlimited long-term capacity, you have a real near-term maximum.*

> *While you have almost unlimited long-term capacity, you have a real near-term maximum.*

We can win almost any battle…

… if we're willing to fight just one at a time.

Guaranteed Success

The sooner we accept our short-term limitation, the sooner we can experience accelerated breakthrough change.

What does this mean?

It means if losing weight is a top priority, focus exclusively on that. Set aside new financial goals. Set aside desires to improve communication in your marriage. Set aside aggressive new goals at work.

If aggressive progress at work is our top priority, set aside weight loss for now.

I know what you're thinking. "How can I set aside those other concerns? If I don't think about those things, they may come back to bite me."

1. This isn't accurate.
2. This fear of focusing is why the vast majority of people do not experience breakthrough change.

> *The hardest thing about creating breakthrough change is not what we have to DO. The hardest thing is what we have to SET ASIDE in order to focus intensely enough to create lasting brain change.*

I said earlier that *Guaranteed Success* is simple. It really is.

But I didn't say it would be easy.

In fact, the hardest thing about creating breakthrough change is not what we have to DO. The hardest thing is what we have to SET ASIDE in order to focus intensely enough to create lasting brain change.

My friend, don't skip this. Don't ignore it.

Embrace it.

It will change your life.

When I fully understood this truth, it hit me hard. I realized that several goals I continually struggled to achieve—including weight loss—had never had my *full attention*. I had always been working on them while working on other things. I never gained enough traction to finish the job and move on. I realized it required total focus: I had to choose one area at a time. Honestly, that was difficult.

Taking this focused approach is worth it. Here's why:

> *Man is not the creature of circumstances. Circumstances are the creatures of men.*
> **Benjamin Disraeli**

1. Concentrating focus is the only way to garner enough focused attention to create long-term brain change.
2. Most results come from automated behaviors anyway—99% of our results will remain the same.
3. Forward progress benefits other areas of our lives. It will have a serendipitous benefit on other areas because it will create clarity and focus.
4. Once new changes are hardwired, we can move on for good. The new level of thinking and acting is now automatic. We don't need to "prop up performance" in that area.

Face reality. Business guru, Jack Welch, believes most mistakes business leaders make arise from an unwillingness to face reality and act accordingly.

The same is true in our personal lives.

We can experience dramatic breakthrough change… if we will focus. Goethe said, "It is in self-limitation that a master first shows himself."

> *It takes about ten years to get used to how old you are.*

Embrace your long-term potential…
   … by accepting your near-term limitations.

Choose. Focus. Decide.
   And be at peace about it.

   Everything will be okay.

In fact, over time, things will get pretty amazing!

> *When trouble arises and things look bad, there is always one individual who perceives a solution and is willing to take command. Very often, that individual is crazy.*
> **Dave Barry**

How long do you need to work on a change?

The answer is simple.

Until you reach the Breakthrough Moment.

If we stop working on a change before then, our gains won't stick. However, if we persist through the Breakthrough Moment, we have it for life.

There isn't a pre-determined amount of time. We need to persist through the Breakthrough Moment. It has been said that if we do anything for 21 consecutive days, it becomes habit. There is nothing magical about 21 days. The magic comes from reaching the Breakthrough Moment!

> *Don't think days. And don't think years.*
> *Instead, think months.*

Whether it takes 21 days, 90 days, or 90½ days, we need to work on a change until we reach the Breakthrough Moment. At that point, we've got it. And the new results that follow the changes will be guaranteed.

Don't think *days*. And don't think *years*.

Instead, think *months*. For larger changes to be permanent, think in terms of around three months.

Here's a brief history of moving from where we are now to the Breakthrough Moment:
1. We learn it. This takes seconds.
2. We do it. This takes intentional focus for around 90 days until it is hardwired.
3. We do it automatically. This lasts a lifetime.

> *Focus long enough so you don't have to focus on it forever.*

Focus long enough so you don't have to focus on it forever.

It's easier than you think. But 90 days feels like an eternity when you're in the middle of it.

But imagine emerging in 90 days different—for good.

In 90 days you will be three months older *anyway*.

> *90 Days From Today:*
> *What will the date be?* _____
> *How would you like to emerge different than you are today?*

The question is:

Will you be *different*?

You can.

Focus.

Relax.

Get in motion.

The Five Stages of breakthrough change

There is a process to *Guaranteed Success*. There is nothing theoretical about it. This is real-world, tried-and-true, meaty stuff. Understanding the process demystifies it. Then we can follow it intentionally, accelerating change and growth whenever we choose.

1—CLARIFY your target:

Goal: Get crystal clear about where you are going next.

Why? You can only hit the target you see.

What you will do: Identify a 90-day target. Include a measurable goal and a performance statement reflecting the person you want to be.

When done: You'll have a compelling and clear performance statement about exactly where you are going next and who you are becoming. You will have made an unequivocal commitment to focus on this target until you reach it.

2—Take daily ACTION:

Goal: Establish the habit of taking tangible action every day.

Why? We can only rewire our brains for lasting change by intensive, persistent, and repetitive action-taking.

What you will do: Establish a daily growth focus time. During this time you will identify one or two tangible ways to move forward toward the target *that day*. You will follow through on those actions *daily*.

When done: You will have an ingrained pattern of daily focus and action-taking that moves you substantially forward toward lasting breakthrough change.

3—Rescript your MENTAL BLUEPRINT:

Goal: Replace your current mental blueprint with a new one to make thinking at the next level automatic.

Why? We habitually act in ways consistent with our most deeply held beliefs about ourselves. If we want to *act* differently, we must *think* differently.

What you will do: Identify your current mental "script" relative to your performance target and then craft a new "script" empowering you to think at the next level. Then turn that script into sets of declarations, and begin reconditioning your mind to think at the next level habitually.

When done: You will have started using declarations on a daily basis to recondition your mind and made substantial progress toward reconditioning your mental blueprint.

4—Upgrade your BEHAVIORS:

Goal: Upgrade a few high-impact behaviors to get results at the next level.

Why? Results come from what we do every day. Two or three small improvements to the right behaviors make a dramatic difference to our performance.

What you will do: Identify top behavioral changes to get results at the next level, and begin ingraining those new behaviors through repetition and mental rehearsal.

When done: You will have accelerated behavior change in the areas that matter most. You will have made substantial progress toward reconditioning your brain to behave at the next level *automatically.*

5—REWIRE your brain:

Goal: Persist through the Breakthrough Moment, where you have hit your performance target *and* hardwired new beliefs and behaviors in your brain.

Why? If we quit before the Breakthrough Moment, we lose most of our work. When we persist through the Breakthrough Moment, changes become hardwired and become the habitual way of thinking and acting, making next level results the "new normal."

What you will do: Persist through the Breakthrough Moment. You will overcome the emotional hurdle of boredom. Persisting through the breakthrough moment is all about patiently "waiting for the cement to dry." Brain rewiring requires focus well beyond the novelty stage.

When done: You will have reached your measurable target and most importantly, you will have rewired your brain to think and act at the next level *automatically.*

That's it.

    Einstein said, "Things must be said as simply as possible—and no simpler."

It's no more complicated than this.

    Let's get started!

Guaranteed Success

Stage 1: Clarify your TARGET

Where next? Why now?

Where do you want to go next?

Why now?

These are immensely important questions.

> We can get just about anywhere—if we stop wandering around and decide exactly where we want to go next.

We can get just about anywhere—if we stop wandering around and decide exactly where we want to go next!

To create lasting change, we must focus more intensely and longer than we are used to. This requires an unusual degree of focus. We will get *bored* before we *finish*. To stay the course, we must believe that our desired result is worth all the effort.

Tim Redmond said, "There are many things that will catch my eye, but there are only a few things that will catch my heart." What captures your heart?

> Why have I survived all these years? First of all, I'm having fun.
> **Michael Dell**

Here are two questions to hone in on:
1. What matters most to you?
2. What should you give total attention to *right now*?

You can't do it all—*right now.*
> You must decide.
>> Where next?

> *If I were to wish for anything I should not wish for wealth and power, but for the passionate sense of what can be, for the eye, which, ever young and ardent, sees the possible. Pleasure disappoints, possibility never. And what wine is so sparkling, what so fragrant, what so intoxicating as possibility?*
> **Soren Kierkegaard**

As you hone in, make sure you choose what matters most right now. You will need every ounce of internal drive to follow through and finish the job.

A Hasidic proverb says, "Everyone should carefully observe which way his heart draws him, and then choose that way with all his strength."

> *You must absolutely believe this is very, very important. Otherwise, you will run out of gas half-way through.*

Only a goal that matters deeply provides internal fuel to keep us going long enough to create breakthrough change. Billionaire Warren Buffett told a roomful of University of Nebraska students, "If there is any difference between you and me, it may simply be that I get up every day and have a chance to do what I love to do, every day. If you want to learn anything from me, this is the best advice I can give you." Make sure you choose a target that can consume you. Everybody is preoccupied. Choose your preoccupation.

Your brain craves an exciting vision. Visionless mission statements do nothing! Neuroscientist John Ratey says, "The intensity with which you attend to such stimuli is determined by your own level of interest, alertness, and anxiety. The cognitive process of assigning an emotional weight to perceptions affects attention as well." The bottom line is that if you don't choose a focus that really matters to you, your brain won't help you achieve it.

So choose something that matters deeply to you.

> *A man is not doing much until the cause he works for possesses all there is of him.*
> **John Wanamaker**

Here are a few tips in choosing your focus:

1. Choose what matters most to you. Everyone—and everything in your life—will benefit most

by this. This isn't selfish—it will ensure that you get it done.

2. Get excited! Anticipate the new results that are right around the bend!

3. Step back. Look at your work and life from a higher place. *Then* choose your focus.

> *Step back.*
> *Look at your work and life*
> *from a higher place.*
> *Then decide.*

Zig Ziglar said, "Life's too tough to get to the top without passion. You're going to fail, be taken advantage of, be disappointed by people you trust, disappoint yourself, run out of resources—almost every day you're going to encounter a good, solid, logical reason why you ought to give up. And without passion, you just might. That's why passion is the prerequisite for peak performance."

I couldn't say it better.

Choose your focus.
　　Stay in your passion.

Steve Jobs said, "Let's make a dent in the universe."
　　Make a dent in *yours.*

> *Hone in.*
> *Be real. Keep it simple.*
>
> *Where next?* _____
> *Why now?* _____

Get crystal clear

Wealth expert Harv Eker points out, "The number one reason most people don't get what they want is that they don't know what they want."

It's time to get crystal clear.

You've identified the area you want to focus on. Now...

...exactly what do you want to do next?

> *This can only mean one thing, and I don't have a clue what that is.*
> **Peter Falk**
> **in Murder By Death**

Here are two questions to bring clarity:

1. *Exactly what new results do you want next?* For example, if sales results are your focus, what is your desired sales number? If weight loss is your focus, what is your ideal weight?

2. *What do you want to become in order to perform at the next level automatically?* For example, if you want to sell at a new level, what new thinking patterns and skills are needed in order to perform at the next level? If your desired results involve weight loss, do you want to cultivate self-discipline with food, or become committed to exercise, or both?

Gaining clarity enables us to keep a goal in front of us in the midst of our immensely busy days. Alvin Toffler said, "You've got to think about the big things while you're doing small things, so that all the small things go in the right direction." When we get crystal clear, that clear target keeps us moving in the right direction.

Clarifying our target is like identifying the Big Dipper out of the vast array of stars in the night sky.

> *When you begin to develop clarity in your future, you become more productive in your present.*
> **Todd Duncan**

Away from city lights, 6,000 stars are visible to the naked eye. Eight stars form a pattern that has been given various names in different cultures over the centuries. We call it the Big Dipper.

Eight stars. To the uninitiated, they are just eight stars among 6,000. To the person who has been primed that there is a constellation of stars that resembles a big ladle, these aren't eight random points of light—they are a picture. Once you've seen it, you notice it every time you gaze into a clear night sky.

> *When you define success, you define relevance.*

When you clarify the target, you identify the Big Dipper of the coming season.

After you identify it, you see it amidst the myriad tasks, opportunities, and distractions of your day. And you can keep moving toward it.

What is your Big Dipper?

Decide what you want. Exactly.

> *Choices are easy when you know what you want.*
> **Lou Holtz**

David Allen says, "Here's a fascinating paradox of the material world: The more specific your vision or intention, the more expansive the creativity you will unleash. The more you know why you are doing what you are doing, the more freedom you have to explore all kinds of ways to get there. The clearer it is why you're having the staff party, why you have a den, why you have an assistant, why the software you are designing is needed, and why you are merging with another company, the more you will tap unique ideas, possibilities, and out-of-the-box options for achieving success."

There are no right or wrong answers. There are just effective and ineffective targets.

Decide. Create an effective target.

90 days to your breakthrough

Think 90 days.

Why?

For two reasons:
1. Life and work flows naturally in four quarters (Q1, Q2, Q3, and Q4) and four seasons (winter, spring, summer, and fall).
2. We can achieve significant brain change in the same time-frame. Larger areas (financial mastery, physical fitness, or an annual sales target) can be broken into focused chunks for a quarter or season. For example, break a one or two year focus on financial mastery into several pieces. These might include defensive mastery (establishing the discipline of living within a budget and trimming spending), establishing solid saving habits, developing strong

investment skills, and creating passive income streams.

Since life unfolds in quarters and seasons, it is useful to work with—rather than against—the natural flow.

> *Since life unfolds in quarters and seasons, it is useful to work with—rather than against—the natural flow.*

A quarter is long enough to experience breakthrough change, yet short enough to keep you from slashing your wrist out of boredom. A quarter is an ideal time for a concentrated focus. Then you'll be ready to turn your attention to something new.

Here are two questions to help you create a 90-day focus. Think about the target you've already identified. Now:

> How might I re-orient and re-clarify the target around this 90-day timeframe?

> *Translate your target into a 90-day time-frame.*
>
> *How might I re-clarify the target around this 90-day time-frame?*
> _____
> _____

What will it take to win?

Here's good news: getting dramatically better results will likely come from doing just one or two things differently.

Here's the tough news: those one or two things will initially take insane discipline to ingrain into your behavioral wiring.

Don't be pessimistic, be realistic. William Arthur Ward said, "The pessimist complains about the wind; the optimist expects it to change; the realist adjusts the sails."

Let's adjust the sails.

Ask yourself—and answer—these questions:
1. What weaknesses have I been unwilling to address?
2. What one or two changes will produce the results I want?

Get ready to adjust the sails.

1. What weaknesses have you been unwilling to address?

_____

_____

2. What one or two changes will produce the results you desire?

_____

_____

Many people are afraid to face reality.

Too often, rather than identifying one or two or changes to be made, they skirt around them, concocting complex strategies.

A perfect example is many people's approach to weight loss.

Weight loss comes down to one thing: consuming fewer calories than we burn. It's no more complicated than that. Yet because many people don't want to discipline themselves to live within a calorie budget, they search high and low for the latest information that will give them some way to lose weight without cultivating restraint. In the end, it all comes down to self-discipline.

Argh! Not that!
Anything but that!

Rather than facing that, people pursue convoluted and complex plans…

… and in the end, end up heavier than before.

Because the real solution is not complicated.

It involves consuming fewer calories than we burn. That requires establishing an iron-clad self-discipline to consume less calories than we burn.

That's it.
>As I said before, it's not complicated.
>But it takes insane discipline to ingrain this into our behavioral wiring.

But we can.
>And in doing so, we will *guarantee* our success.

If I seem merciless toward people who are skirting the real issue in their quest for weight loss, it's because I was there—for decades!

I knew what to eat. I knew that fiber was good, saturated fats were bad. Over the years, at various times I obsessed about fat grams, Weight Watchers points, calories, and glycemic indexes. I exercised, worked at portion control, tried eating more protein, and switched to whole grain foods. I knew it all. I did it all.

But I never won.

Why? Because I lacked impulse control.
>Pure and simple.

I could be "good" for awhile, but not every day. I'd work on it all the time, but never arrived at my desired destination. I thought my ideal weight was just around the corner, but finally realized, "I'm just not getting there!"

It came down to my lack of impulse control.
>Lack of self-discipline.
>Whatever you want to call it.

I couldn't be assured that on a given day I would do exactly what my highest self knew I should do.

Every person who wants to be thin has to meld two realities into one strategy:
1. The need to consume the right calories on a regular basis to assure proper weight.
2. The need to navigate exceptions (holidays, celebrations, vacations,

weekends, etc.).

Strategies break down when they don't meld these two realities together. As I interviewed people who had achieved long-term success with weight, each had a plan that included both of these realities.

I developed a simple strategy to address both of these realities and fully strengthen self-control, so that every day I was in control of my eating choices. It absolutely changed my results!

The biggest secret for me was keeping to my calorie budget daily while navigating the exceptions (like weekends and holidays). I established what I call "The One Rule," where the rule is simply:

> Every day I will count my calories and keep to the calorie budget I established the night before.

This is what I do.
> And it works like a charm.

It has reined in my impulses (I must live today by the decision I made last night) while allowing me flexibility to adjust for special days, celebrations, and events.

Despite its apparent flexibility, the habit was difficult to establish. It took many weeks to establish the iron-clad discipline of keeping to my calorie budget for the day. Why? Because the issue was always *impulse control.* I had to rein in the daily experience of having my brain cry out,

> "That looks good; have it right now!"

Now I can enjoy any of my favorite things—a juicy rib-eye steak and Alaskan king crab, Caramel Cone Haagen-Dazs ice cream, Jones Green Apple Soda, and my sister's oatmeal carmelitas. These foods were never the problem. The problem was a lack of impulse control. Because of that, I consumed too many calories, too often!

Back to the "insane" focus.

It took an *insane* amount of focus to establish the "one rule" discipline. Early on I struggled to stay within my calorie budget. During the first six weeks, I ignored my commitment seven times. But I kept wrestling that sucker to the ground, eventually rewiring my brain so I was in control.

> *The solution is usually quite simple.*

What will it take for you to hit your target? What are the core components of *your* strategy, for *your* chosen target? Again, it usually comes down to just one or two simple things.

Get to the core issue and design the simplest, clearest approach to your target.

If you have hit a sales plateau, why are you capped?
>Be honest.
>Is it your relational skills?
>Are you uncomfortable in certain social settings?
>Do you feel inadequate in dealing with higher potential prospects?
>Are you frittering away time?
>Are you neglecting investment in your personal growth?
>Are you harboring resentment toward people who are outperforming you?

Be honest. This is not about guilt—it is about reality.

Getting new results requires doing some things differently. Remember, a couple small improvements—if they are the right ones—will likely get you the new results you desire.

Be honest. This is not about guilt—it is about reality.
What will it take to win?

What one or two changes would definitively change your results?

Our goals can only be reached through a vehicle of a plan, in which we must fervently believe, and upon which we must vigorously act. There is no other route to success.
Pablo Picasso

Who will you need to become?

Several years ago, my wife signed up for a triathlon.

She set out to *run a triathlon.*
She emerged from it an *athlete.*

Not only that, when the race was over, she was more self-assured and confident in her ability to tackle challenges. The Danskin motto was true for her:
"The woman who finishes the race is not the same woman who began the race."

That is the beauty of establishing and achieving challenging targets.
We emerge different people.

As we think about the new results we want, we want to shift our focus to the person we need to become in order to achieve and live at that next level. When

> *If you change yourself in the process, you will change your results for good.*

we become *that person,* the results we want will be guaranteed. This is the key to *Guaranteed Success.*

Choose a goal for what it will make of you to achieve it.

Dream a little.

Who would you need to become to perform at that level?
Don't try to convince yourself that you can become that person.
Just dream a little.

> *When we do the best we can, we never know what miracle is wrought in our life, or in the life of another.*
> **Helen Keller**

Write a new definition of who you want to become to live at your new level.

> *Write a new definition of who you want to become to live at the new level.*
> _____
> _____

Take a minute to identify why being that person really matters to you. How do you want to be remembered? How might being *that person* influence those who matter most to you?

As I tackled my fitness target, I created a set of mental blueprints called "Why I am fit." Among these is this declaration: "I am fit for my kids." I want my discipline with food to influence my children. Like many families, I have a vegetarian daughter who didn't care much for vegetables and a son who believed the four food groups were snacks, chips, fries, and pop. I want my kids to master healthy eating before they exit our home. Two weeks ago we were having lunch and my daughter set her fork aside half-way through the meal and said, "I'm done." I asked her why, and she said, "Daddy, you stopped eating, so I did too."

That's one reason I wanted to gain mastery with my eating.

Why do you want to grow to the next level?

Why might becoming that person matter to you?

_____

_____

Craft your performance statement

Now it's time to craft your performance statement.

Bertrand Russell said, "The greatest challenge to any thinker is stating the problem in a way that will allow a solution."

There is a world of difference between a goal and a performance statement.

A goal is a target in time. It identifies specific, tangible results to reach by a specific date.

> *A goal is a target in time.*
> *A performance statement defines who you want to be, long-term.*

A performance statement is a definition of who you want to be, long-term.

Both are important.

Let me provide an example of a performance statement. I will use my goal and performance statement for weight loss.

My goal:

> By our Cancun trip I will have the weight off and will have completed my fitness focus.

My performance statement:

> I am exceptionally fit. Every day, without exception, I keep to my calorie budget, overflow with energy, and weigh 149.9 pounds or less!

The goal came and went. The performance statement is for life.

While there is no magical formula for a performance statement, let me walk you through mine as it may yield some insights.

- "I am exceptionally fit"—this is the definition of who I wanted to become. This is how I want to view myself relative to food and fitness.
- "Every day, without exception"—The "day" is the natural time frame in which food choices are made. If I want to be disciplined on *any* day it must be *every* day—otherwise my mind will do what it always used to do; cry out for an exception every day!
- "I keep to my calorie budget"—This "One Rule" that I explained earlier became my "rudder," to stay in control every day while navigating the waters of weekends, holidays, and special events.
- "Overflow with energy"—This reflects a core outcome to achieve through eating and weight maintenance, and it helps me choose foods that fuel me.
- "And weigh 149.9 pounds or less"—I weigh in every night. Alarm bells sound if the scale hits 150! I chose a ceiling (149.9 pounds or *less*) rather than a floor (150 pounds), so I wouldn't "bounce off the floor"—but rather "hit my head on the ceiling."

If that looks well thought-out, it is.

> *Perfection of means and confusion of goals seem, in my opinion, to characterize our age.*
> **Albert Einstein**

Deciding exactly where we want to go next—and who we want to be—is the life equivalent of "measure twice and cut once."

> *When it comes to clarifying where to go in life, it is worth spending time to "measure twice and cut once."*

> *As you craft your performance statement...*
> *1. Make it compelling.*
> *2. Get specific.*
> *3. Be realistic.*
> *4. State it simply.*
> *5. Make sure it clarifies who you will become.*
> *6. Determine your V-Day*

It is certainly worth an hour or two at Starbucks. Or some late night reflection.

As you craft your performance statement, here are some suggestions.

1. *Make it compelling.* It must stir you. In 1961, at the height of the Cold War, John F. Kennedy stood up before the nation and said, "By the end of this decade we will put a man on the moon and return him safely to earth." His words galvanized the nation. Congress unlocked the treasury, many of the best minds created new technologies, and in 1969, his audacious dream became reality. Imagine how different the result would have been had Kennedy simply said, "We're going to beef up the space program." Architect Daniel Burnham said, "Make no little plans; they have no magic to stir men's blood and probably in themselves will not be realized. Make big plans; aim high!"

2. *Get specific.* Exactly what results do you want? Exactly who do you want to be? A Cadillac commercial showed golfers asking a fellow player what he'd shot in the prior round. He sheepishly replied, "Around 71." The guy sitting next to him objected, "You can't shoot *around* 71. It's your score. It's not a round number." Exactly! Get specific. Establish exact dates. Get a digital scale. Calculate to the penny.

3. *Be realistic.* Don't overreach—set yourself up for success. Reward yourself along the way. While you are focusing for a season, you are creating patterns that last a lifetime. Craft a statement that is a possibility for the long-term.

4. *State it simply.* How many Amendments in the Bill of Rights can you name? Did you know there are 27 of them? While I doubt you can name them all, you can easily remember the inalienable rights of man (life, liberty, and the pursuit of happiness). You probably know the original three flavors of ice cream (vanilla, chocolate, and strawberry). The point? Three is a magic number. Keep your focus singular and your strategy simple (three components max) and you'll be clear, focused, and relaxed. Create a brain tattoo.

5. *Make sure it clarifies who you will become.* Remember, the target comes and goes, but who you become stays forever. As you work on your goal, remember to work harder on yourself. This will *guarantee* long-term success.

6. *Determine your V-Day.* When will you be done? For my fitness target, my V-Day would arrive after 21 consecutive days of calorie compliance *and* weighing in at or below 149.9 pounds. I knew all the necessary patterns would be firmly hardwired. When will you be done? Decide now. Look forward to it! If you focus intensely enough, you won't have to focus on this forever. Get in, get it done, and move on!

Okay, craft your performance statement!

> Your past is not your future.
> > A diagnosis is not your destiny.

Decide.

Choose your future.

After you've done it, here's what to do next:

> *Once the idea had formed, I could think of nothing else.*
> *In one weekend I wrote out the concept in incredible deal.*
> **Pleasant Rowland,**
> **creator of the American Girl doll**

My performance statement:

_____

_____

_____

1. Memorize it.
2. Say it ten times a day. Seriously. Start declaring it. See the future *now*.

Your decisions are your destiny. Of all our privileges as humans, none is as weighty as our ability to choose what we will do and who we will become.

Choose your future. Decide your destiny.

Total commitment means total focus

You've decided what you want to do.

Now it's time to commit!

Nobody dabbles their way to breakthrough performance.

This truth may elude us because, after a person masters something, it begins to look easy. But behind that mastery lies intense focus and hard work.

> *Focus is the quintessential component of superior performance in every activity, no matter what the level of skill or the age of the performer. Focus follows interest, and interest does not need coercion. A gentle hand on the steering wheel of attention will suffice.*
> **Tim Gallwey**

This became crystal clear to me when I emailed eight friends who had mastered their weight. One friend had lost 40 pounds several years ago. I knew he'd possess sage wisdom. But he'd never previously let on that losing the weight was a big deal. In fact, several years ago we met for lunch and I mentioned that he looked trimmer. He acted put off by the comment. I wasn't sure how to read his response, but I never brought it up again. It gave me the impression that he hadn't really focused on it—that it had just happened.

> *Every master is a fanatic.*

That was not the case. When I emailed him for insights, he was a wealth of information. He had researched the topic, developed a workable strategy, and actually had an Excel spreadsheet charting his weight loss and BMI.

Like everyone else who breaks through to a new performance level, he was absolutely committed (and fanatical) about it. But to the outside world, he made it look easy.

In fact, I've never met anyone who was really good at something without being somewhat fanatical about it.

My friend, become a fanatic.

We absolutely can achieve much greater results.
But we've got to get serious about it!

What does total commitment look like? Here are some synonyms:

> *To change your brain, your chosen target must occupy your mind.*

- Total focus
- Unequivocal decision
- Singular attention
- 100% of our energy
- Playing to win
- Fighting through to victory
- Focusing like a laser beam

What is the opposite of total commitment?

> *If you chase two rabbits, both will escape.*
> **Unknown**

- Hedging our bets
- Dabbling
- Overreaching
- Juggling
- Spraying and fraying
- Hoping
- Dissipated like a flashlight

Everyone *wants* to be rich but rich people are *totally committed* to being rich.

> *It is possible to own too much. A man with one watch knows what time it is; a man with two watches is never quite sure.*
> **Lee Segall**

Everyone *wants* to be fit but fit people are *totally committed* to being fit.

> *Some people are a jack of all priorities, and master of none.*

Everyone *wants* fantastic relationships but highly connected people are *totally committed* to fantastic relationships.

Every salesperson *wants* to be highly successful but the best salespeople are *totally committed* to being highly successful.

Every leader *wants* to be a level-5 leader but level-5 leaders are *totally committed* to being level-5 leaders.

Turn your want…

… into total commitment.

Cross your Rubicon

On January 1, 49 B.C., Julius Caesar made a total commitment. With the words, "The die is cast," he crossed the Rubicon River with his army, declaring civil war against Pompey and headed straight for Rome.

> *Courage is doing what you're afraid to do. There can be no courage unless you're scared.*
> **Eddie Rickenbacker**

It was a defining moment in Roman history.

It was a *total* commitment. Caesar cut off other options. If he failed, he was dead, but if he succeeded, he was Emperor.

This is a fantastic picture of total commitment.

> *Don't pick a second fight until you finish off the first guy.*

Some simple insights:

1. Never pick a fight you don't intend to win.
2. When you pick a fight, give it all your attention and resources.
3. Don't pick a second fight until you finish off the first guy.

Abraham Lincoln said, "Always bear in mind that your resolution to success is more important than any other thing."

Resolve to succeed.

Do whatever it takes.

Cross your Rubicon.

Fight until you win.

> *It's not until you risk it all and go for the thing you really want that life becomes unlimited. All the shackles are released.*
> **Richard Machowicz, former Navy SEAL**

Guaranteed Success

Stage 2: Take daily ACTION

It all boils down to doing something today

Do one or two great things every day.

You'll get there.

If our target is clear, the key to getting there is chunking away at it every day.

This is so simple we can miss it.

Taking daily ACTION is this simple:

1. *Do something every day.* Don't skip a day. Do something *every day.* Of course, if we occasionally miss a day, we'll be okay. But if we *intend* to miss some days, we will fall off the plan. Be relentless in this! Take *some action* every day!

> *Taking daily ACTION is this simple:*
>
> *1. Do something every day.*
> *2. Don't swing for the fence. Ever.*

2. *Don't swing for the fence.* Ever. It will wear you out. And it won't help. When it comes to brain change, a few big swings won't get you there. The key is continual focus and repetitive action-taking. Save energy so you can do *something* every day.

Consistent, relentless forward movement will bring us to an exciting new place in just a few short months.

> *The secret of your success is determined by your daily agenda.*
> **John Maxwell**

John Maxwell says, "If I could come to

your house and spend just one day with you, I would be able to tell you whether or not you will be successful. You could pick the day. If I got up with you in the morning and went through the day with you, watching you for twenty-four hours, I could tell in what direction your life is headed."

> *All forward progress comes down to "What will I do about it today?"*

All improvement, all forward progress, comes down to...

     ... "What will I do about it *today?*"

Take action.
    Today.

(By the way, reading this book *does* count.)

Establish a time to focus every day

Let's back up.

In the last section I encouraged you to take action every day.

    It seems obvious.

But why *wouldn't* someone take action every day?
    (Because keep in mind, most people don't.)

        Because they are busy.

        Distracted.

        They have stuff going on. Usually *good* stuff.

        You know. Stuff. Life.

The target—the goal—the dream—the possibility,
    which requires some forward movement every day,

        gets buried in the busyness of life.

People intend to do something, but that *something* is small enough to get lost in the midst of daily life.

So how can we set ourselves up to keep moving forward daily?

Establish a time to focus every day.

This is HUGE.

How do we set ourselves up to keep moving forward daily?

Establish a time to focus every day.

This is simple, and it is HUGE.

Please don't skip over it. A daily time to focus may be the single most important habit you establish. If you do this, you are 80% of the way there.

Productivity sage David Allen counsels, "We absolutely must translate long-term goals into short-term deliverables. The possible actions we can take within the next few hours or days motivate and galvanize us."

Here's how:

1. Pick a time.
2. Pick a place.
3. Give yourself 10-15 minutes.
4. Keep the appointment every day.

For me, it is in the morning at Starbucks, on the way to work. During the weekend, I head over to Starbucks near our home and do it before my kids are up. I do it every day (or nearly every day). It has become a daily oasis for me.

If you're resisting this, let me ask a question. If this is not important enough to invest 10-15 minutes each day, are you sure you've picked the right target?

If you've picked a target that really matters to you, isn't it worth a daily investment?

On the other hand, if this matters as much to you as I think it does, it will definitely be worth your daily investment!

Here's what this daily focus time will do for you:
1. It keeps you focused on your target.

> *People that get things done in this world don't wait for the spirit to move them; they move the spirit.*
> **David Schwartz**
>
> *Everything comes to him who hustles while he waits.*
> **Thomas Edison**

2. It provides a place to learn from your experiences.
3. It gives a set time to determine one or two ways to move forward that day.
4. It contributes to the rewiring of your brain (simply by thinking about your target). Daily focus time is, in itself, a form of action-taking. You are fixing attention on the target and changing your thinking and behavior. It is your first form of forward action-taking of the day. It counts.

In fact, it is HUGE.

Establish your daily time to focus.

1. Pick a time: _____

2. Pick a place: _____

3. Pick an amount of time (start small): _____

4. When will you start? _____

What to do during your daily focus time

You've established a daily focus time. Maybe you've cracked the book back open and you're reading these very words during that time. If so, congratulations!

So what do you do during your daily focus time?

First, get a journal. Before the end of TODAY, stop by Borders or Barnes and Noble and pick up a quality journal.

Bring your journal and pen to your daily focus time tomorrow.

Then... what?

1. Focus.
2. Learn something.
3. Decide what to do that day.

That's it.
> But don't let the pure simplicity of it fool you.

> *What to do during a daily focus time:*
> *1. Focus.*
> *2. Learn something.*
> *3. Decide what to do that day.*
>
> *That's it. But don't let the pure simplicity fool you.*

The effects of daily focus time compound quickly. You will be amazed at the progress in just a few short weeks.

Let's look at these three a little more closely.

The first thing we do during focus time is, ummm... *focus.* Focus is accomplished just by having daily focus time. The value of this time can't be overstated. Brain rewiring is happening just by the act of attending to your goal. You've probably heard performance experts say, "Never stop focusing on your goal."

That is what you are doing here! Thinking about your goal, writing down a thought or two, going over your performance statement, or looking at a chart of your progress are ways to fix attention and rewire your brain.

The second thing we do during focus time is *learn something.* When you invest some time thinking about your target, you are making time to think. The daily focus time is an opportunity to become an expert in your target area. Reading a few pages on topic or reflecting on your experiences will

> *You must constantly let go, relax, and refocus.*
> **David Allen**
>
> *Muddy water let stand will clear.*
> **Chinese Proverb**

yield new insights (or reinforce fundamentals) on a daily basis. When you gain an insight, capture it. Create a journal entry. Write it down. Move your brain forward.

The third thing we do during our focus time is *decide what to do that day*.

Let's look at this more closely…

What will I do *today?*

Please remember that by simply investing time daily to focus on your target, you *already are* taking action. That's 80% of it.

The other 20% is taking additional action.

In football, most gains are 3-4 yards. Only a desperate team in a desperate situation runs a "Hail Mary" pass play. Winning teams run plays that gain three or four yards at a time. Every now and then one of those turns into a breakaway play. But most gains are short-yardage gains.

> *You can only gain a few yards every day.*
> *Make sure you gain your yards every day.*

Run a play; gain a few yards.

Remember this: you can only gain a few yards every day. Make sure to gain your yards *every day.*

> *A vision without a task is but a dream; a task without a vision is drudgery; a vision and a task is the hope of the world.*
> **From a church in Sussex, England, c. 1730**

Doing too much can actually be counter-productive. Sports psychologist Shane Murphy says, "You lose effectiveness if you spend too much time on something. Remember that great athletes are always careful not to over train. They work as hard as they can for a practice session, then they stop and rest."

Daily action-taking—continual repetitive forward movement—is the key to creating lasting brain change.

Keep these things in mind as you select an action or two to take today:
1. It doesn't need to be *amazing*—it just needs to be *something*. It's not about *time*—it's about *forward movement*.
2. Don't attempt too much. Think minutes—not hours. Daily action is what matters. The river carries away the mountain grain by

grain.

3. It must be something you can *do, today.* Choose something you can check off.

> *What you do today doesn't need to be amazing—it just needs to be something.*

4. Follow through on whatever you decide to do.

As we begin taking action, it will feel awkward. Every new belief and behavior initially feels awkward.

> *My success evolved from working hard at the business at hand every day.*
> **Johnny Carson**

That awkwardness is to be expected! It is only after repetition that the new patterns of thinking and acting begin to feel natural.

Here are some examples from my journal—each one is simply a journal entry on a particular day:

What I will do today?

1. Learn, think, journal.
2. Begin listing my current beliefs.

What I will do today?

1. Learn, think, journal.
2. Begin a list of potential new beliefs.

What I will do today?

1. Learn, think, journal.
2. Slow down and savor my food and drink.
3. Do my declarations.

No rocket science here.

Just relentless daily forward movement.

> *Fear is success enemy #1. Conquer it by taking proactive action.*
> **Dr. David Schwartz**

You may wonder why I write down "learn, think, journal." I do it so a) I remember that the act of focusing *is* forward movement and b) I can check it off and feel like I've already got one of them done!

> *Action always beats inaction.*
> *Simple action always beats*
> *complex action.*

Short-term goals build our self-efficacy—the sense that we are in control and directing our lives. A Harvard University study found that people who pursue short-term goals gain momentum by attaining their goals more frequently.[7] The amazing Helen Keller said, "I am only one; but I am still one. I cannot do everything, but still I can do something. I will not refuse to do the something I can do."

> *Man stand for long time with mouth*
> *open before roast duck fly in.*
> **Chinese Proverb**
>
> *Close your mouth.*
> *Go catch your duck.*

Napoleon Hill's encouragement is spot on: "Do not wait; the time will never be 'just right.' Start where you stand, and work with whatever tools you may have at your command, and better tools will be found as you go along."

Don't wait to act.
Forget your feelings.

Just move forward.
What will you do today?

> *What will I do today?*
>
> 1. _____
>
> 2. _____

Journaling your progress

Journaling is one of the most powerful ways to collect our thoughts, focus our minds, and chart our progress. Things get specific when we write them down.

Here's why journaling is so potent:

- Journaling accelerates your rate of change. This act of focusing drives brain change deeper, quicker.
- Journaling captures fleeting insights. Gerhard Gschwandtner, the Founder and Publisher of *Selling Power Magazine* told me recently, "Any idea is like a baby. If you nurture it, it becomes strong. If you neglect it, it withers and dies." Journaling helps us nurture new ideas.
- Journaling charts your progress—and this becomes highly motivating as time passes.
- Journaling helps translate your goal into actions you can do today.
- Journaling helps you celebrate wins. Journaling is a fantastic way to savor victories.

When we sit down with our journal during daily focus time, there are many ways to stretch our brain. There are many ways to journal. A few ideas:

> *In the end, it is attention to detail that makes all the difference. It's the center fielder's two steps to the left, the salesman's memory for names, the lover's phone call, the soldier's clean weapon. It is the thing that separates the winners from the losers, the men from the boys, and, very often, the living from the dead.*
> **David Noonan**

1. Create go-forward actions for the day (What will I do today?).
2. Write your performance statement. Write it down, say it aloud.
3. Capture an insight.
4. Capture an idea from someone else.
5. Chart.
6. Evaluate how you are feeling. Do this from time to time to observe the improvements.
7. Call a time out. If something isn't working, stop and ask why.
8. Fix things. Get unstuck.
9. Express gratitude—write down things for which you're thankful.
10. Evaluate core beliefs.
11. Script new beliefs.
12. Dispute a disempowering belief.
13. Write a resolution.

14. Gain insight into personal change.
15. Create some "pull through goals."
16. Gain insight into yourself. In *The Art of War*, Sun Tzu said, "Know your enemy and yourself, and in one thousand battles you will never be in peril."
17. Capture breakthrough memories. It is amazing how we forget important breakthroughs. Writing them down provides future inspiration.

Again, don't over-train.
     Just do an entry or two every day.

Now...
     Go get your journal. Write an entry.

Gain a few yards!

Bouncing back from setbacks

Setbacks happen.
     They are never the problem.

Setbacks only hinder us if,
     because of them,

                    we stop taking action.

"The Great One," Wayne Gretzky said, "I miss 100% of the shots I never take."

Missing shots is never the problem. We all miss!

The problem is if,
     because of our misses,

                    we stop shooting.

Keep shooting.
     Misses happen.

No big deal.

All that matters is that we keep going.

> *Keep shooting.*
> *Misses happen.*
> *No big deal.*

Keep taking action. Keep doing something every day. Keep learning something from every experience.

How to bounce back from setbacks:

1. *Don't sweat it.* Recognize how normal a setback is. David Allen says, "You make mistakes only in a game you're playing."

2. *Learn something from it.* Salvage something. Michael Dell says about the early days of Dell, "We screwed up all kinds of things... Still, we didn't make a lot of the same mistakes over and over again. We learned from the mistakes and figured out how we could progress."

> *I tell each team I coach that we will encounter at least three crises a season. Our success depends on how we react to these threats.*
> **Lou Holtz**

I don't know how many times I have heard people say this. But I still need to hear it! Setbacks *always* sting.

Fifteen minutes before I typed this sentence, I received an email indicating a recently booked six-figure deal might be in jeopardy. In retrospect, there were a couple of small things I could have done differently that might have prevented this from happening. As I encourage you with this, I am reminding myself as well. Setbacks happen. The key is to learn something from it so we'll be better next time (Okay, I feel better just saying it!). I like something Archibald MacLeish once said, "There is only one thing more painful than learning from experience, and that is *not* learning from experience."

3. *Celebrate a partial win.* Don't just be comfortable with it, celebrate it. Destroy the "all or nothing" thinking. Celebrate partial wins and build on them.

4. *Get back at it.* David Schwartz said, "Remember this: how you think when you lose determines how long it will be until you win."

5. *Use action to cure fear.* Kick fear in the butt. Action is always the

best remedy.

I love what wealth expert T. Harv Eker has to say about this: "Rich people are bigger than their problems." The key is not trying to avoid problems. The key is growing ourselves so *we are bigger* than our problems.

The bottom line? Don't worry about failures. Losses are always swallowed up by an ultimate victory. My Seattle Seahawks lost to the Pittsburgh Steelers in the 2006 Super Bowl. After Pittsburgh won, nobody cared that the Steelers barely had a winning record during the regular season. In fact, their earlier defeats—followed by their resilience in the playoffs—became evidence that they were a team full of grit and determination.

> *Losses are swallowed up by an ultimate victory.*

George Washington won only two battles as commander of the American armies in the Revolutionary War. But one of the two battles was the last one—the one that ultimately counted. And that's what we remember. Truly, losses are swallowed up by ultimate victory.

Setbacks only hurt you if you quit.

So don't quit.
     Bounce back.

I'm going to pull out my journal right now and capture a couple insights about how not to jeopardize a six-figure sale in the future!

     What setback can you learn from right now?

Learn from a setback.

Recent setback: _____

What to learn from it: _____

Finish each day and be done with it. You have done what you could. Some blunders and absurdities no doubt crept in; forget them as soon as you can. Tomorrow is a new day; begin it well and serenely and with too high a spirit to be encumbered with your old nonsense.
Ralph Waldo Emerson

Yesterday ended last night.
John Maxwell

Guaranteed Success

Stage 3:
Rescript your MENTAL BLUEPRINT

Your mental blueprint directs your life

In life, we don't get what we *want*. We get what we're *wired* for.

A person strapped with debt says, "I want to get out of this trap." Yet they struggle with the cycle of accumulating it, paying it off,

> *In life, we don't get what we want. We get what we're wired for.*

and accumulating more. They wonder what they'd do when the real estate market stops rising and their ability to reboot their finances goes away. They *want* to break out of the debt trap, but what are they *wired* for? Their mental blueprint is giving them exactly what they are experiencing. They may be wired with thoughts like:

- Living within a budget is restricting.
- My ability to get credit is a sign of financial worthiness.
- I need to own that because so-and-so has one.

We don't get what we *want*, we get what we're *wired* for.

A leader may say, "I want my people to take more ownership." Yet he wonders why he continues getting drawn into projects and issues that shouldn't be on his plate. He *wants* people to take more ownership, but what is he *wired* for? Again, his mental blueprint is the culprit. He may be wired with thoughts like:

- If you want it done right, you have to do it yourself.
- It's really tough to find good people.
- This generation of kids doesn't have the same work ethic.

Guaranteed Success

We don't get what we *want*, we get what we're *wired* for.

A sales professional may say, "I want to grow my sales 10% this year." Yet, she has plateaued. She *wants* higher production, but what is she *wired* for? Again, take a look at her mental blueprint. She may be wired with thoughts like:
- I am already doing everything I can do.
- The market is saturated.
- I'm not sure we really *are* the best value for many prospects.

We don't get what we *want*, we get what we're *wired* for.

A person with 25 extra pounds may say, "I want to be thin." They did the Atkins Diet, the South Beach Diet, and have worked on their weight, on and off, for years. They *want* to be thin, but what are they *wired* for? Check out their mental blueprint. They may be wired with thoughts like:
- Watching what I eat is limiting.
- Being thin is hard.
- I have a sweet tooth.
- When I'm depressed, food makes me feel better.

We don't get what we *want*, we get what we're *wired* for.

In *Secrets of the Millionaire Mind,* Harv Eker uncovers 17 ways rich people think differently than poor and middle class people. If you are working on financial mastery, I recommend this book. Eker makes the point that rich people think like each other. Equally true, middle class and poor people tend to think like each other.

Catch a glimpse of this by looking at the 17 contrasts Eker makes in his book:

1. Rich people believe, "I create my life." Poor people believe, "Life happens to me."
2. Rich people play the money game to win. Poor people play the money game not to lose.
3. Rich people are committed to being rich. Poor people want to be rich.
4. Rich people think big. Poor people think small.

5. Rich people focus on opportunities. Poor people focus on obstacles.
6. Rich people admire other rich and successful people. Poor people resent rich and successful people.
7. Rich people associate with positive, successful people. Poor people associate with negative or unsuccessful people.
8. Rich people are willing to promote themselves and their value. Poor people think negatively about selling and promotion.
9. Rich people are bigger than their problems. Poor people are smaller than their problems.
10. Rich people are excellent receivers. Poor people are poor receivers.
11. Rich people choose to get paid based on results. Poor people choose to get paid based on time.
12. Rich people think "both." Poor people think "either/or."
13. Rich people focus on their net worth. Poor people focus on their working income.
14. Rich people manage their money well. Poor people mismanage their money well.
15. Rich people have their money work hard for them. Poor people work hard for their money.
16. Rich people act in spite of fear. Poor people let fear stop them.
17. Rich people constantly learn and grow. Poor people think they already know.

Please make special note of number three:

> Rich people are committed to being rich. Poor people want to be rich.

Everyone *wants* to be financially successful.
    Wanting does not produce it.
Wiring does.

> *Wanting does not produce success.*
> *Wiring does.*

Every result in our lives—whether great, good, mediocre, or poor—can be traced back to how and what we thought at the gut level.

    Great mental blueprint = great results.

Good mental blueprint = good results.

Mediocre mental blueprint = mediocre results.

Poor mental blueprint = poor results.

Improving mental blueprint = improving results.

Improve your mental blueprint; improve your results.

Peer into the mental blueprint of a sales superstar.

This is from an email sent from Steve Brown, a highly successful sales superstar, to a rookie friend of his. Both are friends of mine so I was "cc-ed" on it. His words of encouragement provide great insight into the mental blueprint of a sales superstar:

"Congratulations on the opportunities you've been successful in developing. Remember, it's a numbers game—the more opportunities, the more chance of success. You will always receive more negatives than positives—that's sales. But if you keep at it, you'll get enough positives to feel darn good about life and your income will increase in proportion to the effort."

Our habitual thoughts do several things:

1. *Habitual thoughts fuel or drain our energy.* Think about how you feel when encouraging, uplifting, and exciting thoughts flood your mind! Contrast that with how you feel when fear, worry, or dread lurk in your mental shadows.

2. *Habitual thoughts predispose us to take particular actions.* The salesperson who thinks a sale is right around the corner is more likely to pick up the phone and make another call than the salesperson that thinks he is struggling and probably isn't going to do a deal today. Thoughts become self-fulfilling prophecies largely because of the actions we take in response to them.

3. *Habitual thoughts shape our interpretation of failure.* Everyone

fails. Often. How we think drastically shapes what we do next: Like all new ventures, our company took quite awhile to achieve "critical mass." During deeply discouraging times, I encouraged myself (and my wife) with the story of Howard Schultz and his quest for capital in the early days of Starbucks. After he pitched his vision, he was roundly rejected by more than 200 potential investors. Even his father asked him, "When are you going to get a real job?" When I was most desperate, I turned to his story and clung to that interpretation of our present struggles. I said to myself, "The greatest ideas take time to catch on. Our vision will catch on—it's just a matter of time. I will hold on and our vision will become reality."

> *A shoe factory sends two marketing scouts to a region in Africa to study the prospects for expanding the business. One sends back a telegram:*
>
> *SITUATION HOPELESS. STOP. NO ONE WEARS SHOES*
>
> *The other writes back triumphantly:*
> *GLORIOUS BUSINESS OPPORTUNITY. STOP. THEY HAVE NO SHOES*

This stage is about how to rescript your MENTAL BLUEPRINT. Specifically, you will:

1. Understand how old ways of thinking created the present.
2. Uncover your current beliefs.
3. Rescript your mental blueprint to produce the results you want.
4. Translate those beliefs into declarations.
5. Learn how to recondition your mind to automatically think at the next level.

> *Getting ahead in a difficult profession requires avid faith in yourself. That is why some people with mediocre talent, but with great inner drive, go much further than people with vastly superior talent.*
> **Sophia Loren**

William James of Harvard said, "The greatest discovery of my generation is that a human being can alter his life by altering the attitude of his mind."

Let's get to work. Let's alter *our* lives by altering the attitude of *our* minds!

You are living a story—whose story is it?

We all live in stories.

You are living a story.

Your story tells where you came from and what your upbringing means. Your story explains what matters to you and why. Your story defines your potential and predicts your future. You interpret every experience by how it fits into your life narrative.

What matters is not what you experience but how you interpret it.

> *The future ain't what it used to be.*
> **Yogi Berra**

Years ago, a popular television show featured the life stories of twin brothers who had grown up in a very dysfunctional home. Their father was a convicted felon. The lives of the boys took entirely different trajectories. One followed in the path of his father—which led him to prison. The other son developed a successful career and happy home life. The most remarkable part of the story was not how *they ended up*, but that they both gave identical responses to the question, "Why did you end up here?" Both brothers, despite ending up in opposite places, gave the same response, "With a father like that, how could you end up anywhere else?"

Same experience. Wildly different interpretations.

To one brother, a horrendous home life meant he had no choice but to replicate his experience.

To the other, a horrendous home life meant doing whatever was necessary to *not* replicate what he had seen.

Same experience.

Two different stories.

You are living a story.

Whose story is it?

Is it reading the way you want it to read?
Is it a boring or exciting read?
Does it make you want to keep reading or take a nap?
Is it turning out the way you want?

It is your story.
    You are the lead character.
    Write it the way you want it to read.

When I was focusing on fitness and weight loss, I became keenly aware of my prior scripting. I discovered an engrained thread of thinking about myself as being stocky. From early in life, I latched onto the idea that I was "stocky," "wide-boned," and "stout." This self-portrait had remained, even during times when I was quite fit. Under the surface, I saw myself as stocky and wide-boned (the implication being that I would have to fight to keep the weight off, whereas narrow-boned people probably have an easier time of it).

> *Memory.*
>
> *False memories. We all have them. Despite great certainty about what we have and have not experienced, given a few bogus details and a little prodding, about a quarter of us can be convinced of childhood adventures we never had. Our memories are much more malleable and fallible than we think.*
>
> *Too often people have taken their view on memory issues as truth. Our improving understanding of memory's constancy, yet flexibility, is opening up windows into how we learn, why we behave the way we do, and how we evolve in our lives...*
>
> *An act of perception is a lot more than capturing an incoming stimulus. It requires a form of expectation, of knowing what is about to confront us and preparing for it. Without expectations, or constructs through which we perceive our world, our surroundings would be what William James called a "booming, buzzing confusion," and each experience truly would be a new one, rapidly overwhelming us. We automatically and unconsciously fit our sensations into categories that we have learned, often distorting them in the process.[8]*
>
> **Dr. John Ratey, neuroscientist**

I never questioned those beliefs. Ironically, I am *not* wide-boned at all. As

I type on my laptop, I see wrists that are actually quite narrow and fingers that are not imposing at all.

As I reconditioned my mind, I dealt with this.

An interesting encounter took place in the middle of all this.

A friend left a message on my cell phone. He said he thought he saw me around town, saying, "There was someone in a car like yours, who looked like you, he was "stout of build..." I literally don't remember anything he said after that. I identified that statement for what it was—false and something I no longer believed. I rejected it. I went into mental conditioning mode, and reminded myself that *I—not he—*am writing my own story. I am *not* stout of build. I am thin, fit, and trim. I am living a story—and *I am writing that story!*

You and I can dramatically change our results, but we must first rewrite our stories. If we want to grow our marriage, increase our net worth, become more connected relationally, or move to the next level in our career, we need to rewrite that sub-plot.

What do you want your story to be?

> Your life is a narrative. You are writing it as you live.

> *Write your own story. You are the main character— so make sure you like the plot line.*

Write your own story.
You are the main character. Make sure you like the plot line.

> *Everything can be taken from a man but one thing: the last of the human freedoms... to choose one's attitude in any given set of circumstances, to choose one's own way.*
> **Victor Frankl**

What is your blueprint set for?

What are you thinking *right now?*

Hit pause for a moment. Really...

According to Brian Tracy, 95% of your emotions, positive or negative, are determined by how you talk to yourself on a minute-to-minute basis.

What are you thinking right now?

Your mind is playing a continuous loop of thoughts. Like background music, it plays in the back of the mind while you are consciously focusing elsewhere. It colors your emotions and shapes your feelings.

Neuroscientists say we have approximately 60,000 thoughts every day.[9]

> *Neuroscientists say we have 60,000 thoughts every day.*

That's about a thought per waking second.

As I type on my laptop...
　　　... let me capture what's running through my mind right now.

- "That breakfast bagel smells good."
- "I like pumpkin spice lattes."
- "Stacy thinks they're too sweet."
- "I like them."
- "I like sweets."
- "Why does that guy keep looking at me?
- "This book is coming along well."
- "Man, this is coming along faster than the last one."
- "I hope Caleb can reschedule our recording time."
- "That Christmas song in the background is slightly annoying."
- "If I have another drink, I'd better have decaf."
- "But it's only 6:28 am; I should wait a little longer."
- "I should move on—this might be tedious for the reader."
- "Or will it be fresh because it's different?"
- "I hope the book is fresh."
- "I wonder what Stacy will think?"
- "Heck, I couldn't get her to read *Stick With It* until after it was

printed."
- "If she doesn't like this, what should I make of it?"
- "Anyway, I better get back to the regular flow."

That was literally my flow of thought (as fast as I could type). Most were simply observations.

You can see how observations can easily take an exit ramp onto a negative side street.

In the past, "I like sweets" could have led to:

- "I have a sweet-tooth."
- "My sweet-tooth always derails my weight loss efforts."
- "Think of how many times I have been good, only to succumb to cravings for sweets that blew my diet."
- "I'll always struggle with this."
- "I wish I didn't have this struggle."
- "I'm powerless to change."

Not too long ago, that's where my thoughts would have taken me.

But I rescripted my mental blueprint.
So can you.

Many of the scripts we have are good. Some are great. Some are mediocre. Some are terrible. The key is recognizing this simple truth:
We don't get what we *want*; we get what we're *wired* for.

Our wiring comes down to two things:
1. Our habitual beliefs.
2. Our habitual behaviors.

And our wiring comes down to two things:
1. Our habitual beliefs.
2. Our habitual behaviors.

Our beliefs—our mental blueprint—shapes how we feel and greatly influences the actions we take or don't take.

Basketball great Michael Jordan said, "Basketball is more mental than physical." Sports psychologist Jim Johnson believes the difference between

AAA ball players and major leaguers comes down to the mental side of the game.

Relative to your current performance focus, what is your mental blueprint set for?

Know this: you are getting exactly what you are wired for.

This is not negative. In fact, it is very empowering! No one else can hinder the improved results you seek. *Guaranteed Success* is simple. Change your habitual beliefs and a few key behaviors, and you get the results you want—guaranteed.

Pop the hood.

What is underneath?

What are your core beliefs relative to this area of life?

This is a very important step in the process of rewiring our brain for better performance.

To uncover your current mental blueprint…

1. Invest your next two or three daily focus times on it.

Luck and Lucky People.

Lucky people expect their interactions with others to be lucky and successful… It is a very simple example of how our expectations can cause us to interact with others in a way that makes our expectations a reality.

Unlucky people have much higher levels of anxiety… Research has shown that people who are especially anxious are often very accident-prone… Anxious people have problems concentrating on what they are doing and are often thinking about their worries and problems rather than about what is happening around them… In addition, other work has shown that such anxiety can affect the body's immune system and can lower defenses against illness. In short, unlucky people's expectations about the future cause them to feel anxious, and these anxieties then cause them to have more than their fare share of accidents and illness.

Lucky people do not dwell on their ill fortune… Lucky people tend to imagine spontaneously how the bad luck they encounter could have been worse, and in doing so, they feel much better about themselves and their lives. This, in turn, helps keep their continuing to live a lucky life.[10]

Dr. Richard Wiseman, The Luck Factor

2. Create a journal entry called "current mental blueprint."
3. Start recording every thought you have related to this performance area.
4. Record everything—without evaluation or judgment. Some beliefs will be empowering, some neutral, some limiting, and some downright negative. Record them all.
5. Give at least two—or three—sittings to this. Make sure almost everything emerges.
6. You should get 15-30 thoughts. Less than 15 means you're probably not thinking deeply enough. But the number is not infinite.
7. Don't categorize them yet. Just capture them.

Here's what I discovered.

Let me share with you—exactly as I recorded them in my journal over three days—what I uncovered about my thinking regarding food and my weight. I share them to encourage you to be real with yourself. Remember, no one else is going to see what you write (unless you decide to write a book and share them with the world!). To re-script our mental blueprint, we must first discover exactly what it is we believe. Here was my mental blueprint:

Food effects how I feel.
Food is fuel.
I've always struggled—I probably always will.
After I'm good for awhile, the cravings will increase—until I satisfy them.
I have a sweet tooth.
I want this food right now (in various settings).
Saying "No" to food urges is difficult and limiting.
I don't know if I can do it.
I'm not in control.
I am overweight.
I am stocky.
I am not a skinny guy—I have a wide frame and could never be a skinny guy.
Some people are skinny—that's not me, never has been, and never could be.
Eating well and staying light is hard.

Current mental blueprint.

1. _____
2. _____
3. _____
4. _____
5. _____
6. _____
7. _____
8. _____
9. _____
10. _____
11. _____
12. _____
13. _____
14. _____
15. _____
16. _____
17. _____
18. _____
19. _____
20. _____

Eating well and staying light is limiting.

Food helps me enjoy downtime, social time, special times, and vacations.

On the surface, I was constantly working on fitness. I exercised four or five times a week—every week. I was obsessive about eating well. I knew almost everything there was to know about antioxidants, carbs, fat, fiber, and micronutrients. At different times I counted calories, Weight Watchers' points, took a low-fat approach in the nineties and a low-carb approach more recently. Many times I set goals and lost weight—only to regain it. All the good things I did (exercising, not getting excessively overweight) sprung from my first two beliefs ("food effects how I feel" and "food is fuel"). Those two beliefs were very positive and kept me working at it.

Overall, though, my results were sub-par. I worked at changing everything, at one time or another. Except my mental blueprint.

Frankly, I had no idea what a mental blueprint was—or how mine was scripted.

> *Changing your mental blueprint is the first order of business.*
> *It will change everything.*

Changing my mental blueprint was the first order of business. And it changed everything.

The first step in changing yours…
… is figuring out what your current mental blueprint is.

Be honest.
>Get real.
>Don't evaluate or judge.

>Just record it.

>What is your blueprint set for?

You are not your thoughts

You are not your thoughts.
>You are your decisions.

This isn't merely positive thinking. This concept is at the forefront of the most recent work in neuroscience.

Some exciting work has been done with people with OCD (obsessive-compulsive disorder). These patients have learned to objectify their storm of intrusive thoughts. Through concentrated mental focus, they have learned to literally rewire their neural connections. Neuroscientist Jeffrey Schwartz has developed breakthrough strategies enabling OCD-sufferers to change their brain. Those who had previously been overwhelmed by flurries of thoughts leading to compulsive activities such as hand-washing were finally freed from their mental anguish. They trained their brains to respond to the electro-chemical impulses by habitually doing something else—like heading to the backyard for some gardening.

A key to their successful mental rescripting came by realizing that their thoughts were not who they were. Their thoughts were electro-chemical impulses of the brain that could be rewired through conscious effort.

Similar work has been done with people suffering from depression. Key breakthroughs come when patients realize depressive thoughts are not who they are, but rather ideas they hold.

> *Our thoughts are not "the way it is." They are "ideas we are having."*

Changing the script from, "This is the way it is," to "This is a thought I am having" makes a huge difference.

Our beliefs are acquired, not inborn.

Our thoughts are something we possess. We can keep them, discard them, exchange them, or acquire different ones.

The beauty of knowing what neuroscience tells us today is that we can choose our thoughts. The ability to consciously choose thoughts and actions is our highest privilege as human beings. You are not your thoughts.

You are your decisions. You choose your thoughts.

Choose the thoughts that will take you where you want to go.

Now that you have examined your mental blueprint, decide what to do with your existing thoughts:

1. Which thoughts do you want to keep?
2. Which do you want to upgrade?
3. Which do you want to discard?

> *File your thoughts.*
>
> *1. Which thoughts do you want to keep?*
>
> _____
>
> _____
>
> _____
>
> *2. Which do you want to upgrade?*
>
> _____
>
> _____
>
> _____
>
> *3. Which do you want to discard?*
>
> _____
>
> _____
>
> _____

Purge the toxins from your thinking

Toxic thoughts.

> They lower our mental immune system.
> They poison our potential.

> *Sometimes we need to learn something new.*
> *Often we need to unlearn something old.*

Sometimes we need to learn something new.

Often we need to unlearn something old.

What is a toxic thought?

Anything that hinders the performance we want. Here are some common ones:

- A.N.T.s—Automatic Negative Thoughts. I can't, I won't, I never do this, I am… I am not…
- Weasel words—Planning to, eventually will, someday, hoping to…
- Mental measles—It's not possible, it's not possible for me…

As soon as we observe a toxic thought, we should purge it from our system. Here's how:

> *Clear your mind of "can't."*
> **Samuel Johnson**

1. Identify it.
2. Objectify it. Do this by writing it down. Getting it on paper takes much of the mystery and permanence out of it.
3. Dispute it. Do this by writing an alternative explanation.
4. Create a new mental script. That's next.

Have a toxic thought?

> Purge it.
> Now.
> Remember, you are not your thoughts.

Purge a toxic thought.

Identify and objectify it.

_____

Dispute it. What is an alternative explanation?

_____

_____

_____

Rescript your mental blueprint

This is one of the most exciting dimensions of *Guaranteed Success*.

To perform at the next level, we first need to think at the next level. When we do this, the rest comes almost naturally.

> *To perform at the next level, we first need to think at the next level.*

What follows will be, I believe, the most practical insight you've ever received on

> *If you want to change the*
> *fruits, you must first change*
> *the roots.*
> *If you want to change the*
> *visible, you must first change*
> *the invisible.*
>
> **Harv Eker**

how to intentionally change how you habitually think.

I am a performance coach, trainer, writer, and keynote speaker. I do intensive one-on-one coaching and keynote speaking to thousands—and everything in between. I read 100 books a year and rigorously apply what I learn to my life and business. What I am going to share with you in these upcoming pages is one of the most powerful tools I can give you to accelerate performance in any area of life or career. Please approach this with an open mind and don't just read it—put it into practice!

There is a great deal of emphasis on how to "think differently." David Schwartz wrote, "You must form an image now of the person you want to be ten years from now if you are to become that image."

But how do we do that?

We have habitual ways we already think. What we think makes sense to us.

While we may catch a glimpse of a better possibility, that glimpse is often fleeting. How do we catch the glimpse for good? How do we rewire our brains to think that new way habitually?

That's what I will provide you now. In the pages that follow, I will provide an intensely practical strategy to rescript your mental blueprint and recondition your mind to think at the new level—automatically.

Some people (not you) might resist this for one of these reasons:
1. It is too simple.
2. It is too much work.
3. It makes them feel stupid.

First, yes, it is simple. It takes some skill, but it is certainly not complicated.

And yes, it is work. But you will find it not a task but a joy. Here's why: choosing to focus on empowering, uplifting thoughts is a refreshing change from the heaviness of the negative thoughts we replace.

Will you feel stupid? Only at first. Everything new feels awkward at first. My "ah-ha moment" came when I realized that I already was talking to myself all the time. And so is everyone else.

By choosing what thoughts I would condition my mind with, I was taking back the mental airwaves! I was choosing what I would say to myself!

At the core, our beliefs are synaptic connections in our brains. We can create new synaptic connections. The catch? This requires massive repetition.
>Knowing a new thought doesn't change our synaptic wiring.
>What does? Repetition of the new thought.

This bears repeating.

Knowing a new thought doesn't change our synaptic wiring.
>What does?
>Repetition of the new thought.

Knowing a new thought doesn't change our synaptic wiring.
>What does?
>Repetition of the new thought.

>Repetition of the new thought.

>Repetition of the new thought.

>Repetition of the new thought.

>Repetition of the new thought.

>Repetition of the new thought.

>>Repetition of the new thought.

> *When the Beatles were depressed…*
>
> *…we had this thing that I would chant and they would answer. It was from a cheap movie they made about Liverpool years ago. And in it they would say, "Where are we going, Johnny," or something and the leader of the gang would say, "we're going to burn this" or "we're going to stomp on that." Well… when we were all depressed thinking that the group was going nowhere… I would say, "where are we going, fellows?" And they would say, "To the toppermost of the poppermost." I would say, "Right!" And we would all cheer up.*
>
> **John Lennon**

Repetition of the new thought.

> *Knowing a new thought doesn't change*
> *our synaptic wiring.*
> *What does?*
> *Repetition of the new thought.*

Tedious?

Maybe so.
That's why many people don't do it.

But knowing a new thought doesn't change our synaptic wiring.

Repetition changes our synaptic wiring.

When you embrace the simplicity of this strategy and the initial feeling of awkwardness, you will discover a tool that is almost magical in its ability to change your thinking and accelerate your results.

When you know how to change your thinking patterns for good, within months you will be able to change the trajectory of any performance area of your life.

Let's get started.

Begin a list. Create a list of at least 15 beliefs. Answer this question:

What must you believe to perform and live at the next level?

There is not a single right answer.

Address the limiting beliefs you had before. Create a potential new list of beliefs to perform and live at the next level.

Don't concern yourself with whether you actually believe them or not. You may not. Just script the beliefs that, if held, would help you live and perform at the next level.

A potential new script.
What beliefs, if held, would help you perform and live at the next level?

_____

_____

_____

_____

_____

_____

_____

_____

You are today where your thoughts have brought you;
you will be tomorrow where your thoughts take you.
Ralph Waldo Emerson

How to create high-impact declarations

Okay, you buy into it.

You see the potential of rescripting your mental blueprint.

You've scripted potential new beliefs.

What's next?

Turning them into high-impact declarations.

Here's where we're going with this. You are going to give yourself the ability to memorize new beliefs and recondition your mind through repetition. While this may sound metaphysical, it actually isn't. It is exactly what we've done to create the habitual beliefs and behaviors we currently hold—we just weren't aware of it.

Now you are taking conscious control of the process, to assure that you condition your mind with beliefs that empower you to think and act at the next level—automatically.

What follows will be extremely practical and specific. It flows out of years of research and hundreds of hours of real-world, in-the-trenches usage.

This powerful tool is available for you. It is ready to go to work for you, today. Here's how to use it:

1. Create sets of four statements each.
Cull through your list of 15-25 potential new beliefs and group them into sets of four. Cluster them in themes. Make sure the four statements are connected in a meaningful way for you.

Why a set? Because our brains remember things in clusters of thoughts, or chunks. Our brains love to connect ideas. Chunk it.

Why four statements? The short answer is that sets of four statements are easy to memorize. To use them for reconditioning, you have to remember them. To remember them, you have to memorize them easily. Four is very easy to memorize.

Several pages ago I shared my mental scripting regarding weight.

One emerging food issue for me was the fear that self-control would be stifling. I needed to assert control AND believe this was a good thing. The tendency to use food for comfort and to boost my mood was something to be reined in.

Here's how I clustered four new beliefs into a set.

Title: "I am in total control"

1. I am in total control!
2. Total control is total freedom!
3. Even in tough patches I am in total control!
4. Food is fuel, exercise is therapy!

2. Keep them simple.
Simple statements are much easier to memorize—and recall.

Think of self-talk in different situations:
- I can do it!
- That's tough.
- We'll figure out a way.
- No way!
- It can't happen.
- I'll make it happen.
- That hurts.
- I love it!
- I'm a fast learner.
- I give up too easily.
- I'm stuck.
- I can change!

Keep your new scripts simple.

3. Make sure the cadence works.
Cadence is the way the statements sound and feel. Like simplicity, cadence makes your declarations easy to memorize and recall. Choose crisp statements that immediately flash in your mind.

Here's an example of poor cadence:

1. I am confident in new social situations and connect with everyone I meet.
2 I like the people I meet.
3. When people are talking, I enjoy what they have to say and listen with my ears and eyes.
4. I learn people's names by repeating them back throughout the conversation and I write them down afterward.

That's obviously a mess. Create a simple cadence that flows. Here's an improvement:

1. I am confident in new social situations!
2. I like the people I meet!
3. I am a great listener!
4. I remember people's names!

4. State who you want to be—not what you used to be.
Instead of "I am not overweight," say "I am thin, fit, and trim."

Rather than "I am not afraid of meeting new people," state "I am confident in new social situations!"

Upgrade "I avoid debt" to "I happily live within my means."

5. Make them present tense.
When you create declarations, you are painting a picture of who you want to be. You are painting a picture and you don't want the picture to be about striving for something. Instead, the picture is one of being the new person.

Don't say "I am losing weight." No one wants to be in weight loss mode all the time! Instead say, "I am thin, fit, and trim." That's where you want to live for the rest of your life. Paint the picture now!

6. Upgrade NOW to level you are going to next.
Your statements need to embody now where you are going next. They don't have to embody your ultimate picture.

Why is this important?

Your mind may rebel against the long-term dream. It is easier to recondition your mind to the next level and build from there than it is to leap to your ultimate destination. Your mind needs to see the possibility.

Recondition your thinking and behavior to the next level. Then build from there.

> *I cannot overemphasize how important your imagination is in shaping your reality.*
> *In a very real way, your imagination helps create the world you live in. You become the person you imagine you are.*
> **Shane Murphy, sports psychologist and author of The Achievement Zone**

7. Put emotion in them.
Use exclamation points! Use great words. Make them succinct, and make sure they "pop" for you. You are painting pictures. Use colorful paint.

8. Create a set for each issue.
As you create clusters of declarations, make sure to create one for each issue.

Remember Einstein's words, "Everything should be stated as simply as possible, but no simpler." In addressing your mental blueprint, you don't need to overdo it. But you do need to address every issue that matters to you.

As I rescripted my mental blueprint for weight and fitness, these were the seven sets I created:

- One for the self-control issue
- One for why I wanted to be fit
- One for seeing myself as thin
- One linking my fitness, wealth, and character
- One about the effects and benefits of my fitness
- One about wanting nutritious food
- One about keeping to my calorie budget each day

I suggest no more than six or seven sets. There are a limited number of issues. Address them all—but no more. The important question is "what do you need to believe to achieve your performance target?" Nothing less—nothing more. Again, keep it simple.

Coupled with your performance statement, you will be armed with a whole new mental blueprint!

One more thing. Don't worry that you don't actually think that way yet. That's the point! You will believe eventually.

Remember, your thoughts are possessions. That's all.

Your decisions are what shape your life. You can change your thoughts by deciding differently. Decide what you want to believe. Condition your mind based on who you want to be and where you want to go. That is who you are at the core—a person with the capacity to choose your own course of action.

Okay, get to work!

Create your first set of declarations!

Potential new declarations on _____ *(theme).*

Ideas:

* _____
* _____
* _____
* _____
* _____
* _____

Refined:

1. _____
2. _____
3. _____
4. _____

Remembering your future

You and I have 60,000 thoughts in a day.

By beginning to memorize and repeat declaration statements, we are taking control of the mental airwaves for several hundred thoughts per day. Rather than being a chore, it will be to the mind what exercise is to the body—refreshing, rejuvenating, and reinvigorating!

> *Recondition your mind to remember your future.*

You know what it will do for you?

It will help you remember your future.

Pure and simple.

We know who we want to be and where we want to go, but we forget. We lose sight of it.

> In our intense and distracted days…
> … it is just too darn easy to get distracted from the goal.

Conditioning your mind with new scripts tattoos the brain with a picture of the future. It helps you remember your future. This will keep you encouraged, motivated, on track, and pushing forward. And it becomes a self-fulfilling prophecy.

Many people hear about declarations/affirmations/confessions, but don't do them. A small number of people write them down. Fewer still say them. And a very small number say them until their thinking is transformed. That is where the real power of declarations comes in. Not in the writing. Not in saying them a dozen times. The power comes in saying them hundreds of times—until the new script becomes the new hardwired way we think. It doesn't happen instantly. It doesn't happen easily. But it does happen eventually—and when it does…

> *Changing our thinking…*
> *doesn't happen instantly,*
> *doesn't happen easily,*
> *but it does happen eventually.*

> …we change.

> We are different.

> Our brain is rewired.

> And new results…
> … are guaranteed.

When you start doing your declarations, here's how it feels.

1. At first, you feel silly and awkward. You're aware you are talking to yourself, thinking, "I am talking to myself. Am I weird?" The beliefs feel unnatural, because they are new beliefs! This feeling is normal. And it will eventually pass. Sound hokey? I love what wealth expert Harv Eker says about this, "I'd rather be really hokey and really rich than really cool and really broke."

2. Then you start feeling encouraged. You start to think it is

> *Doing declarations feels awkward at first. Stick with it. This will change.*

possible.

3. As you keep going, you begin feeling empowered. You see yourself changing. You become aware that you were constantly talking to yourself anyway, and now you're simply choosing your self-talk.

4. Your mental blueprint eventually changes. You see yourself and the performance target differently. It is no longer a stretch. It becomes the new normal.

5. You think differently. Automatically.

When can we do them?

> *Much may be done in those little shreds and patches of time, which every day produces, and which most men throw away.*
> **Charles Caleb Colton**

1. When we first get up the morning. In the shower, brushing teeth, making oatmeal.
2. While lying in bed.
3. Driving/commuting.
4. Waiting in line/at a restaurant.
5. Taking a mental break.
6. During exercise.
7. During dead space (sitting, waiting, in between).
8. While walking.

> *Rule your mind or it will rule you.*
> **Horace**

It's all about rewiring our brains. How many repetitions does it take? There is not an exact number. Think in terms of hundreds, maybe even a few thousand. It won't take a million, but neither will it take a dozen.

It requires repetition over an extended period of time.

The payoff? Eventually the brain yields to what you repeatedly choose to tell it. When the rewiring happens, the new thought pattern will become the natural—habitual—way you view yourself and the targeted performance area.

Austrian immigrant Arnold Schwarzenegger has moved from success to success in his career. His current political success was preceded by two—not one—successful careers. After he succeeded in his career as a bodybuilder, Arnold set his sights on Hollywood. He aspired to become the biggest box office star in the world. Schwarzenegger explains how he leverages his thinking to create his future: "What you do is create a vision of who you want to be, and then live into that picture as if it were already true."

> *Plastic changes in brain representations are generated only when behaviors are specifically attended... And therein lays the key. Physical changes in the brain depend for their creation on a mental state in the mind—the state called attention. Paying attention matters... It matters for the dynamic structure of the very circuits of the brain and for the brain's ability to remake itself.*
> **Jeffrey Schwartz**

Powerful.

Condition your mind to remember your future.

> *Our minds are already preoccupied.*
> *Get preoccupied by your future!*

Now, do it! Start doing your declarations right now!

Do them at least five times a day.

Our minds are already preoccupied.

Get preoccupied by your future!

Guaranteed Success

Stage 4:
Upgrade your BEHAVIORS

Who are your friends and where are they going?

Get ready for a statistic that will startle you.
According to wealth expert T. Harv Eker...

... people earn, on average, within 20% of what their closest friends earn.

Wow!

It's a sobering statistic.

Most of us have scant appreciation of the role environment plays in performance.

More than any single factor, the people we spend time with have the greatest impact on our performance. Dr. David McClelland of Harvard University said, "Our choice of a 'reference group'—the people that we regularly associate with—is the most important determiner of our results." In the *Journal of Healthcare Quality*, Dr. Farrokh Elemi adds, "Creating a positive environment may lead to success even if a person is not fully motivated, because positive environments help the person retain good habits."

Excellence is contagious.
So is mediocrity.

> *Excellence is contagious.*
> *So is mediocrity.*

Energy is contagious.
So is *lack* of energy.

A positive attitude is contagious.

So is cynicism.

There are three kinds of people who affect our performance.

Those who want to pull us down to their level.
Those who want to keep us at our current level.
Those who can pull us up to their level.

Make no mistake about it, the old saying, "birds of a feather flock together," is as true today as ever.

If you want to fly where eagles fly, join the eagles.

Learn from those who know

What I am going to say next may sound harsh.

It isn't.

It's simply true.

Here it is: stop listening to your friends. They probably can't help you.

The quickest way to get to the next level is to close your ears to everyone *except* the people who are currently where you want to go.

This is why so much "peer support" doesn't actually lift us. It makes us feel better, but it doesn't get us to the next level. In our mutual encouragement, we unwittingly propagate the same beliefs and behaviors.

The alternative is to get mentored, coached, and cajoled by people who are actually where you want to go next.

If you want to get rich, learn the lessons of those who are rich. Ignore the financial advice of those who aren't.

If you want to produce in the top 2%, value the ideas of those in the top 2%. Ignore the sales advice of those in the bottom half.

If you want to be thin, glean from the fit. Don't heed the words of the overweight.

If you want a world-class marriage, seek the insight of those who have built world class marriages. Don't listen to people struggling in theirs.

> *It has always been the prerogative of children and half-wits to point out that the emperor has no clothes. But the half-wit remains a half-wit, and the emperor remains an emperor.*
> **Neil Gaiman and Marc Hempel**

While this may seem obvious, remember that misery loves company. And unfortunately, many people opt for company *in* their misery rather than coaching *out of* their misery.

Respect *them,* but give their *opinion* no weight. They don't know how to do it. Only value the opinion of people who have achieved the goal you strive toward.

> *Misery loves company.*
> *Many people opt for company in their misery rather than coaching out of their misery.*

The biggest reason we should only listen to people who have achieved what we want to achieve is simple, elegant, and profound. Because...

...they know it can be done.

If they can do it, you can do it.
> No big deal.
> Yeah, that's right.

> *If they can do it, so can you.*
> *No big deal.*

This is a biggie...

> ... for the #1 obstacle we have to battle and overcome is the feeling that we can't change. People who haven't attained what we seek usually have good reasons for not succeeding. And those reasons will glom onto our minds.

On the other hand, people who have achieved it have reasons *why it can be done.* Their ideas will...
> ... inspire us,

... encourage us,
... fuel us,
... and simply remind us that it can be done. No problem.

When our company was young, Gerhard Gschwandtner, the Founder and Publisher of *Selling Power Magazine* began mentoring my wife and me. Although *Selling Power* is the leading publication for sales professionals in the United States, the company had humble beginnings. Gerhard's sheer determination and work ethic eventually turned the vision into reality. I asked Gerhard how long it took him until he reached profitability. "Five years" was his response. When he recently celebrated the 25th anniversary of *Selling Power*, I told Gerhard over coffee how meaningful his earlier encouragement had been to us.

Gerhard did it. We could do it.

Man, did those words matter when things were nail-biting-tough!

> *Surround yourself with greatness.*
> *Get with people who make you sweat.*

Surround yourself with greatness. Get with people who make you sweat. Invest time with people who pull more out of you and excite you with the potential of your life. Zig Ziglar says, "There is no better way to stay inspired than by spending time in the presence of inspirational people. There is a healthy sort of peer pressure that keeps pushing us forward, a symbiotic effect that causes us to become more in the group... than we could ever become by ourselves."

Groucho Marx was invited to join a high-end Hollywood country club and replied, "I'm not interested in joining any organization that would have me as a member." I like that!

> *Pick people, coaches, and environments that make you feel a bit out of your league. Very soon, you'll find yourself playing ball at their level.*

Pick people, coaches, and environments that make you feel a bit out of your league. And very soon, you'll find yourself playing ball at their level.

My encouragement:

1. Stop listening to your peers.
2. Make a specific list of who to learn from.
3. Go get the information.
4. Spend more time with those people and less time with people who weigh you down.

When I typed this text, the current world population was

6,667,941,040.

That's a lot of people.

Why not *pick* who you invest your life with?

> *To be successful and satisfied in your sales career, you must surround yourself with people who will push, pull, drag, and drive you to greater heights.*
> **Todd Duncan**

Maximize your mentors

Larry Earlywine is one of my life mentors. As I was in the middle of one of my areas of performance improvement, Larry spoke words of life to me. The words stuck in my spirit and imprinted on my mind. I was working hard, but every gain was a battle. Larry simply said this me,

"Greg, this won't always be hard."

Oh my, that was what I needed at the time!

Just getting around people who have done what we want to do is half of the benefit. But we can get much more if we maximize our mentors.

Here are some tips in maximizing your mentors:

1. *Seek out your mentors and coaches.* Go find them—don't take what the cat drags in!
2. *Select them for specific purposes.* Success is specific. If you get access to Trump, ask his advice on wealth, not marriage.

> *Success is specific. If you get access to Trump, ask his advice on wealth, not marriage.*

3. *Ask great questions.* David Schwartz wrote, "Big people monopolize the listening... Top-level leaders in all walks of life spend much

more time requesting advice than they do in giving it." Ask great questions. Dig. Find gold.

> *In times of change the learners inherit the earth while the learned find themselves beautifully equipped to deal with a world that no longer exists.*
> **Eric Hoffer**

4. *Be teachable.* The learn-it-all whips the know-it-all every time. W. Edwards Deming said, "It is not necessary to change. Survival is not mandatory." As I travel widely and work with leaders at all levels, it continues to amaze me how the best are always the most eager learners.

Rose Marie David is an industry-leading District Manager for First Horizon Home Loans. Her Regional President, Curt Altig, and I, designed some recruiting training for Curt's team. Of everyone in the room, Rose Marie needed it the least. Yet she was the most eager learner. She remained for nearly an hour after the program, peppering Curt and me with questions until her inquiries were fully answered. The result? She took her region-leading performance to a whole new level, smashing her own high standards.

5. *Distill the top insights.* When you receive an email from a mentor, read a chapter in a book, or come away from a coaching session, take a few minutes to distill the top insight or two. At one level, capture their spirit and attitude. At another level, distill core insights. Listen to the thinking patterns of champions.

6. *Receive their encouragement.* If they can do it, you can do it. Believe it for *yourself!*

> *It is well to respect the leader. Learn from him. Observe him. Study him.*
> *But don't worship him. Believe you can surpass.*
> **David Schwartz**

Tiger Woods is the greatest golfer in the world.

Yet he is rigorously coached.

Tiger's coach is not the best golfer in the world.

Tiger is.

But Tiger's coach is the best at helping Tiger become *his* best.

Nobel Prize-winning scientist James Watson worked with Francis Crick to crack the double-helix structure of DNA more than half a century ago. He credits part of their success to the fact they weren't the smartest scientists in the room. According to Watson, Rosalind Franklin owned that distinction. The brilliant British scientist was "so intelligent that she rarely sought advice," said Watson. "if you're the brightest person in the room, you're in trouble."

Stay out of trouble.

> Get with smart people.
> Maximize your mentors.

Finding mentors goes against our cultural bias toward the "self-made person." Yet it is the fastest way to accelerate performance. Find people who are at the next level and copy how they think and act. Make those patterns of thought and action automatic...

> *The illiterate of the twenty-first century will not be those who cannot read and write, but those who cannot learn, unlearn, and relearn.*
> **Alvin Toffler**

... and your success at the next level is guaranteed.

Whom will you seek out?

_____

_____

What will you ask them?

_____

_____

When will you do it?

_____

_____

Corrosive influences

Joe Vitale, in *the Attractor Factor,* writes:

> "Visit any bar and what will you hear?
> Gossip. Complaining. Bitterness. Negativity.

Visit any lunchroom in any big company and what will you hear?
Gossip. Complaining. Bitterness. Negativity.

Eavesdrop on any family gathering around dinner time and what will you hear?
Gossip. Complaining. Bitterness. Negativity.

I could go on. The point is, the vast majority of humanity is stuck on this level of consciousness. It's the level of the media. It's the level of most conversations. It's the level of low energy. And this very same level keeps people exactly where they are."

It's true, isn't it?
It's scary.
It's scary true!

Corrosive influences corrode. They corrode our…
… perspective
… thinking
… our belief in what's possible.

Danger.
Beware.

Corrosive influences corrode.

Don't let them corrode *your* mind.

New England Patriots quarterback Tom Brady certainly didn't.

By age 28, Brady had led the Patriots to three Super Bowl titles and was named MVP in two of them. His road to stardom was littered by small-thinkers. When he was available for the NFL draft, the scouting report on Brady read, "Poor build, very skinny and narrow, lacks mobility and the ability to avoid the rush, lacks a really strong arm." Sitting through six rounds, this future-MVP was the 199th player chosen.

His words of advice? "Don't let other people tell you what you're capable of. As long as you believe in yourself and work hard to achieve whatever you set your mind to, you just keep plugging away."

Are any of these corrosive influences eating away at your best thinking?

> *Confidence is contagious.*
> *So is lack of confidence.*
> **Vince Lombardi**

1. Limiting friends
2. Cynics
3. Complainers
4. Justifiers
5. Excusers
6. Trash TV
7. Bad news
8. Trash books

Corrosive influences corrode.
>They cost.
>Big.

Remove a corrosive influence.
What is one corrosive influence I will remove?

_____

When will I do it?

_____

Make simple, powerful changes

Small changes—if they are the right ones—can make an enormous difference. Generally, getting new results comes down to doing just one or two things differently.

To upgrade your behavior, take the same approach you did when you re-scripted your mental blueprint:

1. Identify behaviors that are producing your current results.
2. Cull out one or two behaviors that, if changed, could produce substantially better results.
3. Create one or two new behaviors to learn and hardwire into your long-term memory.

Keep it simple.

> Too controlled is out of control.
>
> Don't make it complex.
>
> We are usually one or two skills away from substantially different results.
>
> Pursue the simplest and quickest path to accelerated results.
>
> Simpler techniques are faster techniques.

Four questions to help you clarify your new behaviors:

1. *Is there a fundamental you have been neglecting?* USA Today recently featured an article on the influx of foreigners into the NBA: "Team-first, back-to-basics foreigners changing NBA." Many home-grown players are neglecting the fundamentals. Sometimes better results are right below our nose. Is there a fundamental you have been neglecting?

2. *Is there something you need to stop?* Sometimes we need to "give up to go up."

3. *Is there a good habit you need to upgrade?* Sometimes we simply need to take something we are doing well, and take it to the next level.

4. *What is the single most important new habit you might to establish?*

> *A nail is driven out by another nail;*
> *habit is overcome by habit.*
> **Erasmus**

> *What single behavior improvement, if made permanent, would have the greatest positive impact on your performance target?*
>
> _____
>
> _____

Keep it simple.

> A small change can make a big difference.
>
> What small change could make a big difference...
>
> > ... for you...
> >
> > ... with your chosen target?

It's all about upgrading your habits

We don't get what we *want*. We get what we're *wired* for.

> Our wiring is our habitual...
> ... beliefs and
> ... behaviors.

Habits of mind and hand.
> Of thought and action.

You grow results by growing yourself.
> Upgrade your habits and you upgrade
> your results.
> Pure and simple.

> *Grow your results by growing you.*

Better habits have incredible potential to create extraordinary performance. Tennis great Ivan Lendl embodied this principle. Lendl was not the most physically gifted player of his generation, but for 270 weeks he was ranked number one in the world. His well-honed habits set him apart on and off the court. Off-court, he cultivated endurance through sprints, mid-distance runs, strength training, and bicycle rides. To increase balance, he engaged in regular ballet bar exercises. He used food as fuel, hewing to a low-fat, high complex-carb diet, and ate at pre-determined times. To stay mentally fresh at tournaments, he instructed friends and family not to burden him with concerns that might distract his focus. Long-time rival John McEnroe said about him, "Much as I may have disliked him, I have to give Lendl credit. Nobody in the sport ever worked as hard as he did.... Ivan wasn't the most talented player, but his dedication—physical and mental, was incredible, second to none... and he did it all through rehearsal."

In *The Power of Full Engagement,* authors Jim Lohr and Tony Schwartz make this comment: "It is perfectly logical to assume that Lendl excelled in part because he had extraordinary will and discipline. That probably isn't so. A growing body of research suggests that as little as 5 percent of our behaviors are consciously self-directed. We are creatures of habit and as much as 95 percent of what we do occurs automatically.... What Lendl understood brilliantly and instinctively was the power of positive rituals—precise, consciously acquired behaviors that become *automatic* in our lives...."[11]

Please don't miss this.

The way people might read Lendl's story goes like this:

"He was an incredibly disciplined person. I'm just not like that."

That's not the message. Lohr and Schwartz hit the nail on the head. Lendl simply developed better habits.

> *Wealthy people are not any smarter than poor people;*
> *they just have different and more supportive money habits.*
> **Harv Eker, author of Secrets of the Millionaire Mind**

Once a habit is developed, the behavior becomes automatic. You and I have thousands of them. Tying a shoe, answering a cell phone, using a fork, and saying hello—these are all hardwired habits.

The key to improving performance is *not* about acquiring super-human self-discipline. It is about focusing effort on the few key behaviors that, if established or upgraded, will improve results. By taking our *habitual behaviors* to the next level, we take our *performance* to the next level—*guaranteed.*

> *Life patterns have a funny way of creating a momentum that is difficult to alter.*
> *You need to take control of your patterns, and not let your patterns control you.*
> **Charles Platkin, author of The Automatic Diet and Breaking the Pattern**

Don't ask...

... What do I need to become perfect at this?

... What do I need to be the best at this?

... What do I need to get to the next level?

That is the question.

A realistic but challenging next level can be attained usually with one or two key behavior changes.

For example,

- a leader wants to galvanize her team to play at the next level. One or two core skill improvements, such as better communication of her vision, might make the difference.

- another leader wants to increase ownership among his people. Again, one or two key improvements, like improving delegation and follow through skills, can make a big difference.

- a salesperson wants to move from the middle of the pack to the top quartile. A couple of skills could lead to breakthrough. Perhaps better time management or stronger ability to generate first appointments after meeting new prospects would create dramatic traction toward better results.

- another salesperson wants to increase sales by 10%. For her, a decision to make one more new prospect call at the end of the day would result in 200 more opportunities—and might put her over the top.

- someone else wants to get the excess weight off for good. Beginning an exercise regimen or counting calories every day—and adhering to a calorie budget—might make all the difference.

- a couple wants to grow their good marriage into a world-class romance. Beginning a bi-weekly date night or having regular chats could be the key. I read an article recently featuring an elderly couple who were a year shy of their 70th anniversary. The article was titled, "Regular daily chat is the secret to 69 years together." In her article, Carol Smith wrote, "Married nearly seven decades, Phil, 96, and Alean, 92, have a simple secret for success. Every day, no matter what, they stop whatever they're doing at 4:30 p.m. to meet for a manhattan and a little conversation. They've been doing it for more than 40 years straight."

This elderly couple didn't list 69 keys to 69 years of marriage. They do a couple of great things consistently. The insight here is not that there is one way to do it, but that a few better habits can *dramatically* improve our results!

Better relationships, better health, better financial results, and improved

> *Better performance is probably just one or two better habits away.*

career success are not 69 steps away. Better performance is probably just one or two better habits away.

Just one or two!

Keep it simple.
> It's less complicated than you think.

Decide what will make a difference for you, and then focus, focus, focus—and make the new behaviors automatic!

And success at the next level is…

> … guaranteed.

What one or two better habits could make a substantial difference over time?

1. _____

2. _____

Train your brain

Repetition is the key to learning.

Repeat the behavior long enough so it becomes hardwired in your brain. When that happens, you will do the new behavior automatically. This will guarantee results at the next level, without having to give it conscious focus. This is the key to lasting, *Guaranteed Success*.

The key is to repeat the exact behavior you desire until it becomes…
> … hardwired
> … automatic
> … something you don't have to consciously attend to.

Focus on this long enough so you don't have to focus on this forever.

Give this intense focus for a sustained period of time so it becomes hardwired and you can perform the better behaviors *without conscious focus* in the future.

> *Focus long enough so you don't have to focus on this forever.*

As we move toward better hardwired habits, there are some stages we will pass through as we train our brain.

> *Train your brain.*
>
> *Six stages we pass through:*
>
> *1. Unaware.*
> *2. Aware of the need to change.*
> *3. Clarifying the new behavior.*
> *4. Awkward.*
> *5. Easier.*
> *6. Automatic.*

1. *Unaware.* Initially, some people are unaware about which behaviors are limiting their results.

2. *Aware of the need to change.* At some point, we become aware of the need to upgrade a behavior or two.

3. *Clarifying the new behavior.* Then we clarify the behavior we want to develop. Remember, there isn't one right way to get better results. A couple may engage in a bi-weekly date night, a daily chat, or employ any of a hundred other strategies. The key here is not *what* we choose to do, but that we choose a better behavior that becomes *hardwired and automatic*. Dabbling at a date night and a daily chat won't help. Hardwiring one or the other so it becomes automatic will make a lasting difference.

4. *Awkward.* As we practice the new behavior, we must overcome the discomfort of feeling dumb. All new behaviors feel awkward at first.

5. *Easier.* After awhile, awkwardness morphs into easier. But don't quit here! There is a huge difference between "easier" and "automatic." If we stop at this stage, the hardwiring is not yet in place. If we stop here, we lose our gains. Stick with it until it becomes…

6. *Automatic.* This is when the new behavior moves from working memory to long-term memory. At this stage we have it for life!

Let's walk through these six stages with a real-life performance area. Say we are working on our finances and want to break out of a high consumption/ debt cycle.

1. *Unaware*: Initially we weren't aware of the gravity of our problem.

2. *Aware of the need to change:* At some point, we became aware of the need to address this nagging issue. Maybe we read a book, heard Suze Orman, or attended a seminar. We owned our situation, declared an emergency, and became motivated to change.

3. *Clarifying the new behavior:* Then we worked diligently to establish a realistic budget and committed to the new behavior of rigorously living within the budget.

4. *Awkward:* Initially, everything in us warred against this self-discipline! Our initial enthusiasm wore off and we found our old brain wiring fighting against the new commitment. It was extremely difficult at first, and we blew it a number of times. But we persisted and kept wrestling that sucker to the ground, and eventually it became...

5. *Easier:* As time went on, living within our budget became the new normal. We found ourselves not having to exert as much effort to do the right thing. We blew it less often. We were greatly encouraged by the improvement. But we didn't take our eye off the ball until it after it became...

6. *Automatic:* This is when it *no longer required conscious focus.* This was well beyond the "easier" stage. At this point we didn't blow it anymore. Our new wiring helped us perform the new behavior automatically. Moving from "easier" to "automatic" didn't take forever. It took about four to eight weeks of continued, laser-like focus.

Allow the words of neuroscientist Daniel Amen to saturate your mind on this:

> Practice does not make perfect. Perfect practice make perfect. The brain does not interpret what you feed into it; it simply translates it. When you are learning to play the piano, the brain doesn't care if you are becoming a great piano player or a terrible piano player. Consequently, if you repeat imperfect fingering, you will become very good at playing imperfectly. If you are training yourself to be a

perfect pianist, it is essential that you practice perfectly and not learn bad habits or sloppy fingering of the keys.... Your brain doesn't care what you give it, so if you care whether you do something well or badly, you must be certain that you are giving your brain the right training.[12]

Please reread that.

Dabbling doesn't do it.
Half-way doesn't help.

In high school, I took typing. Our typing teacher was anal-retentive when it came to not looking at the keys while typing. Most of the class disregarded him when he wasn't looking. Consequently, they hardwired bad typing habits.

> *Cells that fire together, wire together.*
> **Carla Schatz, developmental neurobiologist**

Practice does not make perfect.
Perfect practice makes perfect.

Dabbling doesn't do it.
Half-way doesn't help.

Guaranteed Success is about hardwiring new beliefs and behaviors so we produce new results *automatically*.

Through conscious choice we can remap our brain.

> *Dabbling doesn't do it.*
> *Half-way doesn't help.*

Our brain is a child of our mind.
Our hardwired brains produce our daily actions automatically.
The key to better automatic actions is hardwiring new behaviors.

We can only do that by conscious attention and focus until we have it. Until the Breakthrough Moment.

What's next?

You are aware of the need for a better habitual behavior. What's next?

> *Done regularly, Refocusing strengthens a new automatic circuit and weakens the old, pathological one—training the brain, in effect, to replace old bad habits programmed into the caudate nucleus and basal ganglia with healthy new ones.*
> **Jeffrey Schwartz, author of The Mind & The Brain: Neuroplasticity and the Power of Mental Force**

1. *Script the new behavior.* What *exactly* do you want to do? As I interviewed people who had gained mastery over their eating habits, each person had one or two non-negotiables. They weren't all the same. One person maintained strict adherence to a 1,500 calorie-a-day limit. Another person allowed himself one—and just one—splurge a week. For me, it is keeping to the calorie budget I determine the night before—and doing it *every* day. It doesn't matter which behavior it is. One of many will work. What matters is that the new behavior we choose becomes hardwired and therefore automatic.

> *Your hard-wired behavior will never exceed the behavior you repeat.*

2. *Practice it perfectly.* Remember, practice does not make perfect. Perfect practice makes perfect. You will hard-wire *what you repeat.* Your hardwired behavior *will never exceed the behavior you repeat.* Practice perfectly so you hardwire perfect performance.

3. *Rebound and fix.* For a time, you will blow it. Rebound from those losses. Keep with it. Fix problems. Persevere. Wrestle your brain to the ground! Don't become discouraged. Over time, your brain will yield to your continual conscious choice. Remember, your brain's resistance to change is its way of protecting the habits you've already worked hard to develop. After you persevere and hardwire the improved patterns, it will rigorously defend those new patterns too.

4. *Accelerate through mental rehearsal.*

Use mental rehearsal to speed up the rewiring.

Neuroscientist John Ratey describes how visualizing doing a task taps into the same regions of the brain as actually doing it:

> You are sitting on the couch in your living room. Your friend, seated next to you, asks, "How many shelves are there in that tall cupboard in your kitchen?" You visualize yourself walking into the kitchen, turning your head toward the cupboard, opening the door, and scanning the objects inside, up and down, to help you focus on how many shelves there actually are. You answer, "Four."
>
> To reach this answer, you didn't move a muscle. But you used motor programs, which re-created the movements of going into the kitchen, opening the cupboard door, and scanning up and down. Your brain created motor images—mental simulations of movement—without actually moving.
>
> Research is now showing that you used the same brain regions to re-create this experience as you would have used had you physically gotten up off the couch, walked into the kitchen, and opened the cupboard: the occipital, parietal, and frontal cortex. The purely cognitive process you used to reach an answer was carried out by the regions of the brain responsible for actual movement."[13]

This demystifies the many studies that have illustrated how mental rehearsal improves physical performance. In one study, researchers at Ohio State University divided a group of basketball players into three teams. The teams shot free throws while the researchers recorded the scores. For the next month…

> The first team practiced free throw shooting 30 minutes every day.
> The second team visualized free throw shooting 30 minutes every day (and never physically took another shot).
> The third team did neither.

The result?

After a month…
> The first team improved by 28%.
> The second team improved by 27%.

The third team made no improvement.[14]

Mental rehearsal produced nearly identical results to physical practice. Now we know why: because mental rehearsal activates the same regions of the brain—and therefore hardwires the visualized behaviors—as physical rehearsal would.

Mental rehearsal can help us *accelerate our hardwiring*.

If repetition is the key to learning...
    ... and if perfect practice makes perfect...

        ... then mental rehearsal gives us the opportunity to
            ... get in more repetitions and
            ... practice the new behavior perfectly.

Here are some examples:

- Keeping to a calorie budget. If passing on dessert challenges you most, do ten or fifteen mental rehearsals earlier in the day. Go through the mental process of having dessert offered to you and then responding the way you want. Do this a number of times. It will be as if you had ten to fifteen days of making the perfect choice—and will speed up the wiring process.

- Communicating your vision in a more compelling way. If you have an upcoming meeting with your team, and you want to share your recently clarified vision in a more compelling way, do ten or fifteen mental rehearsals each day leading up to the meeting. Go through the process a number of times. Visualize the room and your team sitting there. Mentally do the presentation the way you will in person. Keep tweaking it until it is just right. Do it several more times. This will speed up the wiring process.

- Fixing a weak sales skill. Every salesperson knows that moving the sales process forward often hinges on better skills at key junctures. I have a sales professional friend who continually saw juicy sales opportunities dry up over five words that emerged over and over again: "Let me poll the employees." This never worked because the prospect didn't know how to adequately present the products. It *always* resulted in a lost opportunity. The sales professional honed a simple but powerful skill to overcome that objection. Earlier in the conversation he would inject, "When I come I will poll your employees…" This one change immediately bumped up his production 25%. To solidify a change like this, identify your better skill and recreate a sales call. Mentally go through the process multiple times until it becomes comfortable. This will speed up the wiring process.

Mental rehearsal is one of the ways to use your daily focus time. Five or ten minutes of mentally rehearsing the behavior you want to ingrain will accelerate the rewiring and move you closer to the Breakthrough Moment.

Try it.

Do mental rehearsal.

Create a clear picture of the behavior you are ingraining.

Take five minutes to do 10 mental rehearsals. Take your time. Thoroughly walk through the process. Remember, perfect practice makes perfect.

Guaranteed Success

Stage 5:
REWIRE your brain

Practice makes permanent

You can get there.
>You *will* get there.
>You *are* getting there!

If you've tried many times before, know this for certain:
>The problem was that you simply didn't persist long enough.

There is no magic to this.
>Just basic neuroscience.

Practice makes permanent.

Period.

Again, please remember…
>… half-way doesn't help.
>… dabbling doesn't do it.
>… it's all or nothing.

Guaranteed Success is about creating lasting, hard-wired change.

We either create it or we don't.

Most of us have been deeply discouraged by past failures. Yet the problem is usually that we haven't persisted through the Breakthrough

> *To find a groove means practice, practice, and more practice.*
> **Wynton Marsalis, jazz trumpeter**

Moment.

There is a Breakthrough Moment for you. There is a point where what you *want* to do will become *easy* to do. At that point, you will have it, long-term. New results will be guaranteed.

But please, please, please, go the whole way. I have found that in the middle of the rewiring process, I get bored. It takes longer than I'd like. What keeps me going is this:

> I want to get in, get it done, and move on.

> I don't want to revisit this performance target later.

I may want to take it to another level in the future, but I don't want to redo this. I've come this far, I want to finish. If I don't finish now, I'll have to redo the whole thing. So I want to get it done *now*.

> *Get in, get it done, and move on.*

Get in, get it done, and move on.

If you are quitting cigarettes, a cigarette never sounds as good as it does when you are in between the old habit and right before your Breakthrough Moment. If you were a two-pack-a-day smoker before, one cigarette wasn't a big deal. After your Breakthrough Moment, you won't want them anymore. But during the rewiring process, while you're going without them—and before your brain no longer wants them—your motivation will wane. You'll feel like it's taking forever, and you will question whether or not the effort is worth it.

> It *is* worth it! Keep going! You are closer than you think! It won't be this hard forever. When you persist through your Breakthrough Moment, you won't want them anymore. If you don't persist, you'll have to start over, and some time, later this year, next year, or in five years, you'll need to restart the entire process again. Don't do it! Get in, get it done, and move on!

Getting a new business off the ground will lose almost all of its appeal when you are between the exciting launch phase and right before the Breakthrough Moment. During the exciting launch phase, you saw no limitations. After the Breakthrough Moment, when the business is off the ground and humming, you will enjoy the compounding benefits of the hard work you've put in. It will be fun again. Launching a business is only fun at the beginning—when we are ignorant—and after we are profitable. But for a year or two or three in between, it feels like we are peering into the void. During that time, it feels like it's taking forever, and you question whether or not all the effort is worth it.

> It *is* worth it! Keep going! You are closer than you think! It won't be this hard forever. When you persist through your Breakthrough Moment, you will enjoy it again. If you don't persist, you'll have to start over, and some time, later this year, next year, or in five years, you'll probably want to try it again. Don't quit! Get in, get it done, and move on to the next level with your business!

Feeding frenzies will never be as appealing as they are in between old habits and right before the Breakthrough Moment. If you ate whatever you wanted before, no single splurge was a big deal. After your Breakthrough Moment you won't want to throw off the restraints anymore. But during the rewiring process, while you're wrestling your eating urges into submission—and before your brain gives up the fight—your motivation will wane. It will feel like it is taking forever, and you will question whether or not the effort is even worth it.

> It *is* worth it! Keep going! You are closer than you think! It won't be this hard forever. When you persist through your Breakthrough Moment, you won't want fatty, artery-clogging, energy-draining foods anymore. If you don't persist, you'll have to start over, and some time, later this year, next year, or five years from now, you'll start this process over again. Don't do it! Get in, get it done, and move on!

If you don't persist...

... you will eventually be back doing this again.

Period.

> *Persist.*
> *If you don't, you will likely be back doing this again.*

127

If you don't want to do this again later, keep going! Get in, get it done, and move on. Finish it!

> *The only way to change people's minds is with consistency.*
> **Jack Welch**

In the middle of every rewiring process, I come to a moment of truth when I've been working on the target for a long time and the victory stills seems distant. I always to come to the point where I have to decide:

Am I going to get it done now?

The decision that moves me beyond is this:

"If I don't do it today, I won't do it *any* day.
I don't want to have to come and do this again—I am finishing it now!"

Like you, I have so many things I want to accomplish, contribute, achieve, do, experience, become, acquire, and give away. Oprah Winfrey said, "I have come to realize that you can't do everything at once." If I am going to go after other targets, I need to nail this one right now.

To accelerate our lives, we need to finish what we're working on right now. Get it done. Then move on. Without this approach, we will be dabbling at this level forever.

No!
Not that!

Let's get in, get it done, and move on!

Cross the chasm.

Continue.
Finish.
Persist through the Breakthrough Moment.

When your brain is rewired, what you *want* to do will be *easy* to do.

Five words of encouragement:

1. *It will not take forever.* There is a specific point where your brain shifts learning from working memory to long-term memory. This is not esoteric. It is literal, physiological change that makes thinking and acting at the next level automatic.

> *Five words of encouragement:*
> *1. It will not take forever.*
> *2. Avoid the temptation to turn away too soon.*
> *3. Practice makes permanent.*
> *4. Finish.*
> *5. Always remember that once you get it, you've got it—for life.*

2. *Avoid the temptation to turn away too soon.* You've carefully laid the forms and poured the cement. Now let it dry.

3. *Practice makes permanent.* What you focus on expands. We have all experienced it; now neuroscience explains why it happens. Results are temporary; habits are lasting. Make permanent the habits that guarantee long-term success.

4. *Finish.* Determine now that you will *never* come back and redo this! Determine now to stick with it and get it done!

5. *Remember, once you get it, you've got it—for life.* Hold on to this when you feel like quitting.

> *Sustaining attention is the primary gateway to encoding memories.*
>
> *When complex motor tasks become routine they are pushed down to the subcortical areas, where they reside as more automatic programs. Once a procedure is stored in this lower memory it becomes hard-wired. That's why we can get on the proverbial bike and pedal away after a decade of not riding. If these skills had stayed in the higher cortex and been unused, the connections would have withered and been lost. Adults who gave up their rock-'n'-roll bands in high school find that when they pick up a guitar years later they can still play…*
>
> **John Ratey, neuroscientist**

> *Results are temporary.*
> *Habits are lasting.*

129

Here's a big question:

How long will you persist?

There are three possible answers. Pick yours.

How long will you persist?
_____ *1) I'm done for now. I'll come back to it later.*
_____ *2) For _____ more days.*
_____ *3) Until I finish.*

How long?

So how long?

> How long does it take to hardwire the new beliefs and behaviors?

Simple answer.

> Until we pass through the Breakthrough Moment.

You can make mistakes, even some big mistakes, and still prevail. That's a wonderful thing to know.
Jim Collins

Never give in, never give in, never, never, never, never—in nothing, great or small, large or petty—never give in except to convictions of honor and good sense.
Winston Churchill

Press on. Nothing in the world can take the place of persistence.
Ray Kroc

Two truths:

1. It doesn't have to be any longer.
2. It can't be any sooner.

Play to win. Not to avoid losing.

When rewiring the brain, here are three basic stages to remember:

1. Awkward
2. Easy
3. Automatic

When we move from awkward to easy, *we are not there yet.* We're half-way there. Most of those who persist through the awkward stage, mistake the "easy" stage with the "automatic" stage. If it's not automatic, it's not rewired yet. If we quit before it's rewired, we'll lose most of our gains.

> *What this power is I cannot say; all I know is that it exists and it becomes available only when a man is in that state of mind in which he knows exactly what he wants and is fully determined not to quit until he finds it.*
> **Alexander Graham Bell**
>
> *Most of the important things in the world have been accomplished by people who have kept on trying when there seemed to be no hope at all.*
> **Dale Carnegie**

Move from awkward…
    … to easy.

Persist from easy…
    … to automatic.

Be careful.

When things get easier, it means you are getting better results.

The sting of earlier poor results diminishes. Losing 20 pounds feels great! But if our goal was 40, it is easy to become lax and not finish. Be aware that your present pain will subside and then it takes pure grit, determination, and desire to persist through the Breakthrough Moment and get it done for good.

> *Move from awkward…*
>   *… to easy.*
>
> *Persist from easy…*
>   *… to automatic.*

Keep your mind on the goal: *Guaranteed Success.*

The goal isn't a lessening of pain.

Or improved temporary results.

Your goal was—and is—to make succeeding at the next level *automatic.*

Let me ask the earlier question again.

> *How long will you persist?*
> _____ *1) I'm done for now. I'll come back to it later.*
> _____ *2) For _____ more days.*
> _____ *3) Until I finish.*

others considered boring—and it led to extraordinary performance game after game.

Making free throws is exciting.
Mastering free throw shooting is boring.

Excitement for our performance target gets us going.
But we must apply grit and determination to persist through the boredom stage.

How long does this take?
Maybe two extra weeks. At most two extra months.

It certainly won't take forever.
But persisting through the Breakthrough Moment requires it.

And remember, when we do…
… we have it. For life.

> *There is nothing brilliant or outstanding in my record, except perhaps this one thing:*
> *I do the things that I believe ought to be done…*
> *And when I make up my mind to do a thing, I act.*
> **Theodore Roosevelt**

Your V-Day!

What is V-Day? It is the day you declare victory!
It is the day you celebrate the new performance target becoming your new normal.

It is the day you have achieved your target and can move on.

Many people never plan their V-Day.

For one reason.

> They don't believe they'll ever get it done.

It is a core limiting belief.

> This perception—as much as any other—keeps people from pouring themselves fully into their goal. If we believe it can be done, we will give it all we've got. V-Day *will come* if we give it all of our focus. So plan it! Get excited for it!

Many people never plan their V-Day.
For one reason.
They don't believe they'll ever get it done.

Believe this one thing:

> You absolutely can—and will—win.

Plan your V-day.

Three questions for you:

1. How will you know when you will be done?
2. What is your target date to finish?
3. How will you celebrate?

Make it real.

Play your V-Day.

1. How will you know when you will be done? _____

2. What is your target date to finish? _____

3. How will you celebrate? _____

That target date *will* arrive.

Will you focus, make the sacrifice, and be different when that date arrives?

Water boils at 212, but at 211 degrees, it's just hot water.

> Keep the heat on!

> Make the sacrifice.
> Finish.

"I'm not asking you, I'm telling you. These creatures are the only sentient race in the sector and they're made of meat."

"Maybe they're like the Orfolie. You know, a carbon-based intelligence that goes through a meat stage."

"Nope. They're born meat and they die meat. We studied them for several of their lifespans, which didn't take too long. Do you have any idea of the lifespan of meat?"

"Spare me. Okay, maybe they're only part meat. You know, like the Weddilei. A meat head with an electron plasma brain inside."

"Nope, we thought of that, since they do have meat heads like the Weddilei. But I told you, we probed them. They're meat all the way through."

"No brain?"

"Oh, there is a brain all right. It's just that the brain is made out of meat."

"So... what does the thinking?"

"You're not understanding, are you? The brain does the thinking. The meat."

"Thinking meat! You're asking me to believe in thinking meat!"

"Yes, thinking meat! Conscious meat! Loving meat. Dreaming meat. The meat is the whole deal! Are you beginning to get the picture, or do I have to start all over?"

Live the life you've imagined

Life.

> What a privilege.
> What a responsibility.
> What an adventure!

How much life do you have left?

The average lifespan is eighty years. If you live to eighty, here's how many minutes of life you have left:

Age Now	Minutes Left Until 80 Years Old
25	28,908,000
30	26,282,000
35	23,652,000
40	21,024,000
45	18,396,000
50	15,768,000
55	13,140,000
60	10,512,000
65	7,884,000
70	5,256,000
75	2,628,000
79	525,600
79 years 11 months	43,200
79 years 11 months 30 days	1,440
79 years 11 months 30 days 23 hours	60
79 years 11 months 30 days 23 hours 59 minutes	1

A month ago I was thinking about the weekend in front of us. My kids are growing up fast. My thirteen-year-old daughter has only 250 weekends left in our home. My 12-year-old son, 300.

Sobering, isn't it?

It's like cold water on the face.

There is no time to waste!
> Life matters.
> It is an adventure.
> And it is fleeting!

Give your all to what is present. Albert Camus said, "Real generosity toward the future consists in giving all to what is present."

Live with all your might. On January 5, 1919, at his home in

> *The great French marshal, Lyautey, once asked his gardener to plant a tree. The gardener objected that the tree was slow growing and would not reach maturity for one hundred years. The marshal replied, "In that case, there is no time to lose; plant it this afternoon."*
> **John F. Kennedy**

New York, Teddy Roosevelt died while he slept. Vice President Marshall said, "Death had to take him sleeping, for if Roosevelt had been awake, there would have been a fight."

Don't hold back. Heed Abraham Maslow's powerful words, "If you deliberately set out to be less than you are capable, you'll be unhappy for the rest of your life."

Cultivate excellence. Aristotle's words ring through the millennia, "We are what we repeatedly do; excellence then, is not an act but a habit."

Make your contribution. Jesus' words, spoken five centuries after Aristotle's, put our good things in perspective, "To whom much is given, much is expected."

Strive for greatness and encourage greatness in others. Pablo Picasso said, "My mother said to me, 'If you become a soldier, you'll be a general; if you become a monk, you'll end up as the pope.' Instead, I became a painter and wound up as Picasso."

Autograph your work with excellence. "Every job is a self-portrait of the person who does it. Autograph your work with excellence." Anonymous.

Complete your mission. Richard Bach, in his book *Jonathan Livingston Seagull*, is asked "How will I know when I've completed my mission?" The answer? "If you are still breathing, you are not done."

> Don't bulldoze over life's moments. Savor them.
> Enjoy the game you're in.
> Reach higher.
> Make today count.
> Exceed you.
> Stop needing and start leading.
> Live your adventure.
> Build a greater life.
> > For you. For others.
> > > Make your difference.

Live the life you've imagined!

Notes

1. *Think Thin—Be Thin:* Doris Helmering and Dianne Hales (New York: Broadway Books, 2005), p. 1.
2. *"The Neuroscience of Leadership," Strategy + Business Magazine:* David Rock and Jeffrey Schwartz, Issue 43, Summer 2006, pp. 72-73.
3. *A User's Guide to the Brain:* John Ratey (New York: Random House, 2001), p. 179.
4. These are drawn from the works of John Ratey, Jeffrey Schwartz, Pierce Howard, Daniel Amen, Richard Restak, and Joseph LeDoux.
5. *A User's Guide to the Brain:* John Ratey, p. 94.
6. *The Mind and the Brain—Neuroplasticity and the Power of Mental Force:* Jeffrey Schwartz and Sharon Begley (New York: HarperCollins, 2002), p. 130.
7. *Breaking the Pattern:* Charles Platkin (New York: Red Mill Press, 2002), p. 152.
8. *A User's Guide to the Brain:* John Ratey, pp, 56, 183-185.
9. *Think Thin—Be Thin:* Doris Helmering and Dianne Hales, p. 11.
10. *The Luck Factor:* Richard Wiseman (New York: Hyperion Books, 2004), pp. 108-110, 134.
11. *The Power of Full Engagement:* Jim Lohr and Tony Schwartz (New York: The Free Press, 2003), p. 166.
12. *Making a Good Brain Great:* Daniel G. Amen (New York: Crown Publishing, 2005), p. 119.
13. *A User's Guide to the Brain:* John Ratey, p. 147.
14. *The Magic Lamp:* Keith Ellis (New York: Three Rivers Press, 1996), p. 53.

Contact the author

Greg Wingard can be reached at gregw@simpleteamsolutions.com